Anna
Blake

Relaxed
& Forward

Relationship Advice from Your Horse

Author photo by Sheri Kerley
Cover photo by Anna Blake
Cover design and formatting by JD Smith

Published by Prairie Moon Press

All enquiries to annamarieblake@gmail.com

First published 2015

ISBN: 978-0-9964912-2-8

For my Ghost Herd:

They are as visible as earth and sky, as stark as night and day, and as real as skin and bone. I don't remember my grade school teachers, but I remember the horses who were in the pasture. I knew we were friends because when we walked together, they were careful to keep their heads very low, just level with mine, so we could hear each other. They taught me how it works: You have to let your heart be soft. You have to let your love be just an inch bigger than your fear.

Not More Riding Lessons...

"How long do you think you will have to take lessons?" Twenty years ago and I can still hear that tone in my mother's voice. She wondered why her adult daughter—after a life of riding—would need lessons. How hard could it be? I forced a smile as I checked my heart for knife wounds, and reminded her that Olympic riders all had coaches. Mom gave me an eye roll.

Does someone give you that eye roll? Sometimes it's easier to get defensive than try to explain hundreds of lessons in a lifetime of riding. Each horse and each rider are individuals, forming a unique pair—and the conversation begins. Trust is offered shyly at first, maybe the horse responds well to ground work and a connection is established. Then we mount up, trusting them to hold us safe, as they trust us to choose a safe path.

At some point, it gets more complicated; someone gets scared, frustrated, or intimidated by the naked honesty a horse and rider display. There's a hesitation; and in that quiet moment, a sensitive rider understands that they have come up short in some area. In that same moment, they become aware that the horse has held faith in them. In some physical or emotional way, the horse has given them the benefit of the doubt and the hook is set.

It is humbling to have a horse hold the door open to a sacred place, and wait for you to enter. It makes you want to do better, to be deserving of the respect he has shown you.

So a rider might continue to take lessons, not from an

inability to learn, but a desire to improve, fueled by respect for an equine partner. Riding is sometimes like interpretive dance, creative and spontaneous. Lessons can spark ideas and help translate our desire into direction. Growing pains aren't comfortable for horses or riders. We can look like we need therapy for a dozen maladies, but our horses inspire us on toward some sacred, addictive place of oneness with them. And so we persist.

"Press on. Nothing in the world can take the place of persistence. Talent will not. Nothing is more common than unsuccessful men with talent. Genius will not. Unrewarded genius is almost a proverb. Education will not. The world is full of educated derelicts. Persistence and determination alone are omnipotent." —Calvin Coolidge

Who's Spookin' Who?

It was time to take my proud and extremely green Arabian gelding out of the arena for the first time. We were wandering about the barnyard and I was confident in my negative thinking—certain bad things were waiting to happen. Then my gelding spooked big, staring at a spot on the ground in front of him. I tensed and leaned to see what had scared him. He kept staring and so did I. I asked him to move to the side so I could have a better view, and then in our new position he stared at a different place on the ground—even more nervously. Nothing was visible—no plastic bag, no snake, nothing but dirt.

Now I was hooked, what *was* he looking at? Eventually I saw it. There was something in his shadow that he hadn't seen before: me riding him!

This is where I am supposed to make fun of my young Arabian being afraid of his own shadow. Instead, let's make fun of me. I was afraid of something I couldn't even see until it dawned on me; then I was afraid of MY own shadow! How scary is that?

Arabians are great teachers of crisis management and we grew to be brave partners. The memory of the spook has lingered; it was a humbling moment. It's so easy to get caught up in our horses' drama. When they need us to provide calm leadership the most, it seems human nature to tense up and look for the scary thing. We might as well all be preteen girls screeching at skeletons in a haunted house! BOO!

When we let the external confusion take precedence over our inner wisdom, we aren't much help to anyone. Focus is a challenge but this is where riders could take a cue from moms.

They frequently have a *deal with it now and cry about it later* sort of mentality that makes them valuable in a crisis. And since horses like to feel safe in the hands of a focused and confident leader (a good mom), it is an easy analogy.

Personally, I don't like being referred to as my horse's mom—I know the mare and she deserves credit. Instead I would like moms and riders both referred to as Boss Mare. It's a title that comes with respect.

On Horse Movies:
Velvet Brown Lied

It's the movie *National Velvet*—and a twelve year old Elizabeth Taylor lied. *The Man from Snowy River* came a bit closer, but still fell short. Don't even start with me about *The Horse Whisperer*. These are beloved horse movies, watched by horse-crazy girls and boys of all ages. By definition, movies require a suspension of disbelief from the audience.

My point is that when the rider, Velvet (or whoever) leans forward and whispers into the horse's ear, The Pi (or whoever), that part isn't real. Whispering into a horse's ear isn't actually what wins the Grand National. Months of daily training are abbreviated into an ear whisper to move the story along. Even when riders know it's consistency and commitment that move a horse along, most of us harbor a National Velvet fantasy well past midlife.

I love horse movies—as I rewind and replay, I get inspired. In real life, the race is never won in a few moments. Horses require riders to be so conscious physically and authentic emotionally that there can be no ego or deception. It takes work; the dream isn't free.

Sometimes Hollywood gets it right. My pick for best real-life horse movie is *Seabiscuit*. It isn't romantic—parts are gritty and ugly. Jockey Red Pollard says, "You know, everybody thinks we found this broken-down horse and fixed him. But we didn't. He fixed us; every one of us. And I guess in a way, we kinda fixed each other too." Still saccharine for sure, but I think that's how it works.

For professional riders or amateurs, in handicap riding programs or elite equestrian facilities, (and especially this week at our little farm) the experience is the same. Riders are mired deep in challenge and uncertainty, and sometimes out of their comfort zone—but pushing on. There are no miracle cures and no matter where we start, riders each seek their personal, Grand National version of oneness. Horses inspire that in riders and artists and just about everyone else.

It wasn't true when Walt Disney said that a prince on a white horse would ride up and rescue us either. But some of us went out and got white horses (or brown ones or orange ones), and rescued ourselves. Princes can take forever to get here, but horses can start today. A horse is an affirmation we can strive to be worthy of; working with them makes us better people. We might even inspire princely behavior in others and gasp—they might make a movie...

The Problem with Perfection

Lots of us riders are perfectionists. It isn't a bad thing to want to get things right. We want the best for our horses—the best care they can have for their health and wellbeing into old age. We want to be the best riders we can so that their work is easier and more beneficial.

Lots of us were raised by parents who wanted the best for us and sometimes showed it by acting as if nothing we did was good enough—or that's what we heard. Again, there's nothing wrong with wanting to get things right, unless our critical side is the loudest voice. That negative back-talk can suck the joy out of riding pretty quickly.

Horses have a simple approach to life. They don't think about your Olympic dream or your physical shortcomings or the stress you feel at work. They do think about green grass while they are eating it or how good a dirt bath feels after a run. They live in the moment, and then they get over it and live in the moment again. Horses have an enviable freedom from self-judgment and guilt.

Perfection is a frozen and limited place, usually a line to fall short of. However, art is easy and possible in questing spontaneous moments. String a few of those moments together and it might be better than perfect. It could verge on brilliant!

On a good day there is a gift we can give our horses. We can help them glory in the physical feeling of their body—strong and balanced—moving fluidly with a rider who asks with kind leadership and rewards with generosity. In return, we can be carried weightless, in a place above past regrets and future worries. All we have to do is let go of our mental meanderings and join our horse in the present. There is a quiet ecstasy in paying attention.

Ram Dass isn't quoted nearly enough in the horse world—he says, "Be here now." I am sure he meant to also say it's the rider's shortcut to better-than-perfect.

From a Whisper to a Scream

"Hit him!" If I am not yelling, I am certainly speaking in a loud, firm voice. How did it come to this? The answer is easy; I need to rescue a horse from a long-winded abuse of kindness.

Let's start at the beginning; loving horses is fine, but they don't care about that. Horses will choose respect over love every time. Understanding herd dynamics is crucial for a rider; to partner with a horse, we have to share a (non-verbal) language. Respect is their primary herd language, learned from Mom on their first day. So step one for a rider is to give up speaking English and learn the language of horses.

The situation that has given rise to this rant was watching a series of various riders try to get their horses moving forward. Kicking (nagging) a horse every stride trains him to be dull and deaf, then riders become stiff and frustrated. Nagging is a sure path to mutual despair.

There is a misnomer about horse whispering—you don't always whisper. I like how Tom Mowery describes it, "You be as rude as they are." Instead of bickering with your horse, be a kind leader and stop threatening him with the whip—actually pop him once. When there is a consequence to his apparent deafness, hearing improves. He will be grateful for the clarification and make a better choice next time. Then ride on happily as if it never happened, without a grudge.

Nagging your horse into a stupor is a different kind of abuse and it insults both parties. A horse is a proud, smart partner and if you cue him as if he is disabled and dim-witted, he will behave that way. The kind thing to do is give him a tap with your whip and show him that you respect him enough to ask consistently for his best.

Horses have always been my best teachers, requiring a perceptive level of asking and listening. One horse had a habit of kicking me in the arch of my foot if I over-cued him. On the other hand, if he was being lazy and I would give him a quick correction, he would exhale and let me know it was fair. It was his way of saying I might be *ambition-impaired* but I am not stupid.

Let the Real Treat be You

When I was younger, I always carried sugar in my pocket because it felt so great to have my horse come to me. It was cheap vanity—until the inevitable day that I forgot to fill my pocket. My gelding stood on my five-year-old foot, begging for a treat I didn't have. I was pinned—without enough muscles or brains to move him back. He started to get more aggressive and finally I wiggled my tennis shoe out from under his hoof. My trust in him was as bruised as my toes. Sugar has a darker side!

It is easy to know who the alpha horse is in a pen—just toss an apple in and see who gets it. What we might call food aggression is just common sense in the herd. We give treats to dogs as a reward for a behavior. Dogs find out the treat isn't free and they happily comply with the command—it's a fair trade and a door opens to understanding and working together.

Feeding a thousand-pound horse a treat without exchange of behavior is a different thing entirely. Horses don't care that *you think* you are giving it, they just take it. No debate. You might even think that your horse is being affectionate when he is doing a body search for more food to take. Your vanity is rewarded, but dominance is also settled. You've lost and you aren't tacked up yet.

Exceptions exist, some horses aren't as food motivated as others, and some riders are smart about treats. Herd dynamics are complex and horses frequently understand more than we are aware. I choose to not hand feed my horses—call me cruel, but I still remember not having the currency when I needed it. Most of all, I want to evolve my leadership beyond food as the only reward.

A few weeks ago, my horse fell with me while cantering. He got hung up in the fence while getting up, took a nasty scrape to the groin, and scared himself pretty badly. (I was fine.) Nubè was at the end of the arena, shaking, by the time I got to my feet and clucked for him. He swung his head toward me and trotted back with a huge blow upon arrival. He didn't come to me for a treat; he knew I had something he wanted more.

Good leadership is the best treat for a horse, and apparently, a rider can still be vain about it!

Hard Hats and Hard Heads

The helmet debate continues for riders, especially of my generation. It flares up when well-known competitors or local friends get injured. After the incident passes the debate continues at a quiet level.

I will be honest; I am late to the helmet wearing side of this debate. Before, I wore them for some events or on some horses, but not consistently as I do now. Lots of us do it that way—judge some situations as helmet-worthy. Obvious times are on young horses or while jumping. We think youth should wear them, but we hesitate to set the example. Maybe we think helmets make us look afraid or geeky.

Ironically, buying trainer's insurance decided the debate for me. I read in black and white in the policy that I was responsible for the safety of others. It got personal; I thought about how I would feel if one of my horses hurt someone, and it grew from there. All situations became helmet-worthy from that vantage point. It followed that I should set the example with concern for my own hard head. And eventually, I got to be proud of my choice to make no exceptions to the helmet rule at my barn. I got here a bit backward, but now I never ride a step without a helmet.

Don't misunderstand: I am a giant fan of personal choice. I don't like having laws to tell me how to dress. I just wish wearing a helmet was everyone's personal choice.

Sometimes I wonder if making the helmet decision on a

case-by-case basis isn't more dangerous than not wearing one at all. When I see my peers wearing hats for photo opportunities I wonder if that is the part-time helmet message they mean to send others. Special occasions should be the time we wear helmets especially.

My youngest student is proud to be wearing a helmet with her half chaps and boots. It is part of the badge of honor to be a rider. Everything about adults is more complicated and not necessarily better. I do know this for sure; horses are addictive, complex creatures, who are nearly irresistible. Ride forward, do your best, and please, take very good care of what makes you who you are. You'd be lost without it.

Riding as Meditation

Riding can be a form of meditation in the best sense—a release from day-to-day drama and worry. It's amazing how much better the air is just a few feet above the ground, and moving through the air at a trot really does give you the feeling that sheets get blowing dry on a prairie clothesline.

It's easy for a rider to lose that clean sheet feeling. Some riders carry their work stress with them to the barn. Others lay down their work stress and pick up riding stress: fear, frustration, impatience, unrequited desire, ego, or just plain overwhelm at all the awareness and skills that conscious riding requires. Horses will let you know that justifiable stress is still stress.

We talk a lot about focus in lessons. For our purposes, focus means the ability to stay mentally present and physically balanced in the saddle in a quiet and conscious way, while life goes off around you. It takes practice to stay conscious and consistent in an unconscious and inconsistent world.

External situations are not always controllable, but we do have something to say about internal distractions. We all make riding mistakes and beat ourselves up about it. Humility can easily become low self-esteem, and that will destroy our focus from the inside out. We betray the trust our horses give us if we abandon them in favor of our own fears of inadequacy.

We should treat our own selves with the same kindness and understanding most of us have for our horses. It's common sense simple that horses like happy, focused riders. Learning to put our mental demons on a sit-stay while we ride takes practice.

The best advice I have read lately about keeping positive focus was not in a book about riding—it was in *Bird by Bird*, a book by Anne Lamott about writing. I highly recommend this book to riders. Riding and writing are even more alike than they sound.

Lamott quotes Geneen Roth, *"Awareness is learning to keep yourself company."* I like this definition; it has a peaceable, friendly sort of invitation to it.

Lamott adds to that, *"And then learn to be more compassionate company, as if you were somebody you are fond of and wish to encourage."*

In other words, treat yourself like you would a horse.

Strong Words for "Weak" Riders

I was at a dressage show earlier this season and overheard two women talking about a rider they both knew. "She isn't driving the horse onto the bit; she just isn't *strong* enough to drive him to the bit!" one said with a sharp edge to her voice.

My heart sinks when I hear comments like that. It gives dressage a bad name, just like similar comments do with every other riding discipline. It doesn't reflect well on us riders; sometimes we just try too hard and end up being adversarial with our horses (and ourselves).

We have all seen riders who try to control a horse with strength—grunting, red faced, and tense with exertion. Does she actually think it's possible to push a thousand pound horse forward with a force of human strength, and still maintain a relaxed, round horse? The quality of the gait is tarnished by tension and force is never a good substitute for finesse.

I could rant on long into the night. Instead, I suggest going to YouTube and search for a Bill Woods video of Dr. Reiner Klimke on BioTop, (Aachen, 95). Klimke, at 59, riding with energy and finesse in a warm up arena. Responsive, rhythmic, and above all, without coercion.

Horses truly do want the lightest cue possible. If the rider gets tense in the asking, the response from the horse will be tense as well. Worse yet, if a rider allows tension to join up with gravity, the horse will give a dull, dense response. The nagging begins and the possibility of a joyous dance instead becomes dull work. Unhappy rider equals unhappy horse. *"Do not conquer the world with force, for force only causes resistance."* —Lao Tsu

Too often riders equate energy with emotion; when energy goes up, it turns into anger or frustration. There is another choice. Instead, let light, positive energy percolate in your torso; adjust your inner thermostat without attaching an emotion to it. Practice an inhale and dial up your energy with transitions forward, then exhale and cool the energy to come back. Breathe, *allow your energy to be elastic,* and your horse will return the favor—happy response from soft cues.

Conscious riding is challenging; it takes mature patience and mental focus to learn the fundamentals. But once we understand, we should let the mental effort settle and ride with the child-like enthusiasm of a horse-crazy girl. Or Dr. Klimke.

Making Little Girls Cry...

The gate opened and in came the first horse/rider combination. The horse was a post-prime Arabian, trotting quickly with her nose out. She was groomed to a shine, with a braid in her mane already beginning to fray. The rider was a tiny girl in jeans, rubber tall-boots and a scuffed helmet. I think she was wearing her very best school sweater.

I had been enlisted to judge a year-end show at a friend's barn. Nothing too elite here, the riders in her program were thrilled to ride lesson horses.

The rest of the class entered, similar riders on similar horses, and I went to work. At first glance you could think these riders were kind of pathetically cute—compared to the *real* horse show world. In other words, all the heart but not many advantages.

But the air was tense, and these riders were very serious. They sat tall and centered in their saddles with heels down and focus up. They deserved my full attention, and if I made any of these girls cry, I would have to kill myself.

Disclaimer: I'm not a judge. I do use my perception to train and I believe that judgment is an art. I was always taught that it was a cheap shot (and the lowest measure of intellect) to look for faults, especially from a seat in the stands. Identifying failure is easy, but that means counting mistakes to eventually reward the least-bad ride. Instead, I was taught, "Look for what you like." Affirming moments of brilliance takes the adversarial edge out of judgment.

We all worked hard, and by mid-afternoon, we were all exhausted, especially a certain chestnut horse who had been shared by two riders. He was just done; now he resisted every cue and tossed in a few bucks for spice. His rider held her position, and soldiered on, red-faced with effort and embarrassment. It was a really rough ride—the kind that builds more character than ego. And I had to pin them last.

I caught this rider's eye as she rode out of the arena. She stopped, still sitting tall. I put a hand on her horse's neck and congratulated her; she'd handled a challenging ride with good sportsmanship. I told her it was a job well-done and for the first time, big tears fell. *(Just kill me.)* But I watched her ride out and by the time she got to her mother, she was smiling and chattering. She bounced off, and hugged her horse.

Lots of folks hate competition and it's complicated to explain why I value it so much, but some of it involves little girls crying.

Zappa and Einstein:
Riding Out of the Rut

Here at Infinity Farm we are riding in a rut—literally—a rut runs along the rail of the arena. The first definition of rut in the dictionary is "a sunken track or groove made by the passage of vehicles." Most arenas have ruts. Every week I do Zamboni work on the sand, but a rut is always just below the surface. That rut is how I know we are riding in a rut figuratively. The second definition of rut in the dictionary is "a fixed, usually boring routine." One rut defines the other.

Some riders tell me in a self-congratulatory way, "My horse hates arena work." They imply that the view from a dressage saddle is tantamount to watching paint dry. To tell the truth, when I look at a trail literally, it seems to fit both definitions of rut as well.

I don't think it is *where* we ride so much as *how* we ride. Horses and people are creatures of habit and gravity encourages our default position to be one of comfort and familiarity. At the same time, horses and people are creatures who bore easily.

"*Without deviation from the norm, progress is not possible.*" —Frank Zappa.

This week in my lessons I decided to shake things up a bit. I took the reins and steered my students out of our usual rut. Initial resistance gave way to progress!

"Imagination is more important than knowledge." —Albert Einstein.
The best riders I know manage to keep their horses (and clients) interested by being creative and fresh every day. It takes energy to be creative, but soon the combination of the two becomes a positive, self-sustaining circle.

In diversity and unity, both Zappa and Einstein came from a foundation of knowledge to say that creativity makes all the difference. If creativity was so important in their worlds, then it must be doubly important in our world, partnering with the spirit and grace of horses.

The time change this weekend heralds in the dark months when plenty of smart animals hibernate. Or at least ride that way, in ruts deep and frozen. It's the time our horses really need us to crash the rut; you could get a trainer's input, crank up the music, cross train, or just elevate your riding conversation above repetitive small talk.

Let deviation and imagination be our new winter rut!

When I Die, Can I Come Back as Your Horse?

I've heard that line a few too many times. I guess it's meant to be funny. I was flattered once when a vet introduced me that way but think hard. It might not mean what you think it does.

The least flattering time I heard this reincarnation plan was while I was rubbing mineral ice on my horse's inner thigh. He had torn a muscle and was in his second month of stall rest. The man who said it thought he was Columbus discovering the New World, and a total laugh riot. Arf, Arf—my humor was lost a week into our forced rest and recuperation.

It isn't that I was unaware of the humor in my compromised position, especially if it isn't your hand and your horse. But like I said, I was humorless that day. Instead I went mental!

Could he *really* want to come back as my horse? You know there is more to it than mineral ice and carrots, right? Are you willing to work hard day after day, season after season, year after year? Can you commit to that? Can you be that vulnerable physically and emotionally? Are you willing to build a trust so deep that it will carry the two of us as high and light as a thought? Will you hold my life as strongly and gently as I hold your life? When all is said and done, will you try one more time? Will hearing me say, "Good boy!" make you try even more? Do you *really* want to be my horse?

(Whoa! Do I sound like Jack Nicholson in *A Few Good Men*?)

Reconsider, Brother. Mineral ice isn't expensive. By the time dreams and commitment work their way into reality and all the surface trappings fall away, what's left is precious. Trust is something some of us riders and horses take pretty seriously.

"At its finest, rider and horse are joined not by tack, but by trust. Each is totally reliant upon the other. Each is the selfless guardian of the other's very well being." —*Author Unknown*

You would have to be pretty ambitious to want to come back as my horse. I think it might be smarter to come back as my cat. Or better yet, my goat: now there's a lifestyle you could kick back and enjoy. And I know they would appreciate your sense of humor.

Beauty—Redefined from the Saddle

"Life should NOT be a journey to the grave with the intention of arriving safely in an attractive and well preserved body, but rather to skid in sideways, chocolate and wine in one hand, body thoroughly used up, totally worn out and screaming "'WOO HOO what a ride!"

The first time I saw this quote it was on a Maxine greeting card but the idea originally came from a passage by the one and only Hunter S. Thompson. Either way, it has always had a *barn battle cry* feel to me—with the vehicle being a horse.

So many images of beauty in our culture seem to be about being weak; teetering in high heels, wearing restrictive clothing that limits natural movement, and spending hours primping. Still we never quite measure up to the celebrity-survivors of plastic surgery and air brushing, who are our cultural icons of beauty.

It's a no-win situation—eventually we all get old. But what if we had a different standard and instead beauty was a reflection of strength and confidence, made more valuable with years of polish?

What if it was obvious to everyone that a woman moving in unison with a thousand pound horse was more beautiful than a woman wearing *Versace* on a red carpet? (Wiki definition: The experience of "beauty" often involves the interpretation of some entity as being in balance and harmony with nature, which may lead to feelings of attraction and emotional well-being.)

Or a big smile under a riding helmet was considered sexy? Or men were wildly attracted to women that horses and dogs liked?

What if the guilty pleasure was watching a TV show about four Amazon equestrians who didn't live in NYC and wore dirty Ariats instead of Manolo Blahniks? Would it be the worst thing if riding instructors were universally respected and cosmetic plastic surgeons were shunned as fringe-dwellers?

And since this is obviously *MY* fantasy—what if old legs could still dance. Every day older we became, the sum of our beauty would continue to grow. Pasty teenagers would look at us with awe and respect as (did I mention this is a fantasy?) we arrive loud and proud, skidding in sideways—wrinkled, used up and howling!

"I want to grow old without face lifts. I want to have the courage to be loyal to the face I have made." —Marilyn Monroe.

Dear Drama Queen

Dear Drama Queen,

I understand you getting upset. You have so much passion and desire for riding. I know how hard you try to be the very best. Sometimes the world seems to conspire against you; it's like every bad thing happens to you and none of it is your fault. No one else has to cope with your unique situation, and no one understands. On top of that you feel bad when you don't get the respect you deserve.

Sometimes it happens at a horse show. It's a stressful time and there are always extenuating circumstances. Some judges are blind or simply not very bright. You say it isn't fair.

Feelings get big at horse shows, but sometimes it happens at home too. Everyone else is so self-important; they are all rude and impossible to be around. There are days when every effort fails and a saint would cry. Life is hard.

I understand—literally. I have my drama queen days too. Sometimes I'm cranky and hormonal, and don't like anybody. Sometimes I'm confused and stressed out, and don't know which way to go. Sometimes I just feel like stomping my feet and throwing my head back and screaming. Being a drama queen is very satisfying. Period.

The problem with being a drama queen is that it really impacts others. You aren't always aware of it but I see it. It changes everyone's mood; less laughing, more tension. People look away and don't make eye contact. I think they talk about you later. It isn't about whether you are right or wrong; people are just uncomfortable with the conflict and want it to stop. They end up holding a grudge, can you feel it? Even the dogs avoid you...

But not me, I stand with you. On a good day, you and I are undeniable, beautiful partners sharing the same shadow.

But when you get angry, frustrated, or any of those dark thoughts, I'm still your partner. I feel every part of you tense up. I get embarrassed and nervous for you. Is it my fault, did I do something wrong? Why are you ignoring me? I worry, I don't want to be a bad horse.

Sorry to sound like a drama queen about this, but it really does hurt me the most...

Signed,
Your Partner

Who Am I This Time?

Who Am I This Time is the name of a short story written by Kurt Vonnegut and made into a film with Christopher Walken and Susan Sarandon. It's a quirky story about two people of very different and uncomfortable personalities who fall in love while acting in a community theater production of *Streetcar*. (Hear Walken's painfully shy, tongue-tied character roar, "Stella!!" during the play within a movie. He is remarkable.) I continue to be a Vonnegut fan *unstuck in time* and travel back into his writing frequently.

I am reminded of this particular story while working with horses and riders; it's the question horses ask each time a different rider climbs on. Who am I this time? Do I care to listen? Can I be lazy? Is this a substitute teacher or she-who-must-be-obeyed? Or the best question; can I dance with you?

Most of us have the experience of mud-wrestling with our horse until we are too frustrated to breathe, only to see our trainer ride that same horse like an Olympic hopeful. Most of us know horses like the mare I rode as a child; she routinely tried to kill grown men but treated me like treasure.

If it wasn't so humiliating it would be easier to respect our horses for their ability to accept each rider without assumption. Horses aren't fooled by expensive breeches or big talk in the barn aisle. They simply see us for who are as riders. He may be a Grand Prix horse but if you are training level, well, there you are.

Horses are brutally honest. I think it's their best quality. In a world of actors and roles to be played, I know exactly where I stand with horses. I may not always like it but I do trust it.

But wait! It was Shakespeare who said, "*Assume that virtue though you have it not.*" He knew a thing or two about acting. Maybe acting like a good rider is a start.

Sometimes our personality isn't the best match for where our horse is at the moment but acting the part of a confident rider might begin a change from being the *Odd Couple* to Fred and Ginger in *Shall We Dance?*

Do you have a *Tom Hanks* of a gelding? Maybe he'd do better with a *Meg Ryan* rider, rather than a *Church Lady* rider. Can acting the part of a happy, enthusiastic *Meg Ryan* sort of rider really be considered dishonest?

Do you have a *Meryl Streep* (in any role she ever played) sort of mare? Is it too much to ask to be a *Katherine Hepburn* (in any role she ever played) sort of rider?

Who are *you* this time? Who do you want to be?

Helmets and Freedom

A friend of mine volunteered at a nursing home. One of the patients there was always talking about riding and my friend thought that maybe I could come along and talk horses with her. That was what I knew when I entered her room.

The walls were covered with horse pictures from magazines, a couple of medical machines were humming and sighing, and there was a stuffed horse-toy on the bed. She was lying facing the wall, quietly crying. I asked if I could come in, and as she turned, I was surprised to see she was half my age. I'd expected an elderly person. I forced a smile and asked if she liked horses.

In the next few minutes she repeated the same story several times; she had a horse, he was beautiful, she had ridden all her life. Sometimes she remembered her horse's name, sometimes not. Then she'd start again—she had a horse, he was beautiful... She continued to cry off and on. It was hard to tell if her pain was physical or mental, or if that even mattered. There was no doubt she had been a serious rider. And then she would remember again, she had a horse...

I don't know the extent of her injury, but it was severe, chronic, and the result of a riding accident. I don't know if she was wearing a helmet. She had been there over a year; her young husband came as I was leaving.

I'm not sure this tragedy is mine to tell but I know I'm haunted by the visit. The truth is that she reminded me of myself as a little kid. Like her, I stared at pictures and longed so deep for a horse that I moaned. I was possessed with my desire, it ruled my days and nights. Once she was just like me—we could have ridden together. Now she is held captive in the hurt of wanting and not having, with a child's mind that doesn't comprehend.

Until I met her, I didn't *understand* there was something worse than losing a horse.

Riders know all too well the risks that come with horses—every day, every ride. We weigh desire with risk and we don't like to think about injury. I've written about the helmet issue before, but there's has been more talk recently on the heels of the Riders4Helmets Helmet Safety Symposium. While opinions rage on both sides of this debate, I have been remembering the trip to the nursing home.

I can't choose for you, but I know me—I will never be okay with not riding; that pain would never leave me. I may end up in that same nursing home room eventually, but in the meantime I'll use every brain cell I have to be safe as possible in my world of risk. If wearing a helmet might buy me more time on my horse, then it buys me freedom.

Equine Gastric Ulcers… and Sage

I'll call her Sage.

I have changed her name to protect the guilty. It isn't that I think the guilty deserve protection, but this isn't their story. The story I want to tell is about this beautiful mare and me.

Sage was a thoroughbred mare with classic elegance. A solid bay with an elegant long neck and pointy withers. She was very feminine, not too tall, but she was proud.

That's who she was born to be but what she looked like was very different. The first time I saw her was in a small stall showing every ulcer symptom in the book, loud and clear. This mare was not stoic; her pain was obvious and hard. Anyone could tell she was in distress. Sage had ulcers and she was screaming for help.

Sage had been given to a riding program for retraining after repeatedly injuring her previous owner.

She was not mine to train, she was not mine to help. She was none of my business.

I bit my tongue for a while. When I did speak to her trainer in private she didn't disagree with my assessment. Over the next few weeks she looked just as uncomfortable as the first day. Her coat was like sandpaper. I was told the ulcers were not treated, but she was under saddle with a new owner. Later, I broke professional boundaries and spoke to her owner as well, with no success for Sage.

I saw Sage and her owner again, this time at a clinic for

troubled horses. After a dangerous hour the clinician said he felt Sage could never be *normal* under saddle.

He's right; training can't heal a physical condition, like lameness or ulcers. Our first responsibility is to make sure that a horse's resistance isn't a result of a physical issue. Sage wasn't given that help.

I got a call for a favor when Sage colicked and I agreed to haul her to the clinic. Have you witnessed the pain of colic? Her *normal* pain didn't prepare her for this. She fought courageously and the vet did his very best. I was holding the lead rope while Sage was euthanized. At the very end, I did help her with the pain.

Sometimes we do everything we can to help our horses and we lose them anyway. It's a small comfort to know we tried. I did not have that satisfaction with Sage.

She was not mine to train, she was not mine to help. She was none of my business.

I'm thinking of Sage as I prepare to give a talk on Equine Gastric Ulcers at an Equine Education Day this weekend. I have a lot of experience helping horses suffering from ulcers and I bring it up every chance I get in clinics and lessons. Statistics say over sixty percent of performance horses have ulcers, so victims aren't hard to find.

Some folks are probably tired of hearing me try to spread the word about managing ulcers. Maybe they think, "Who died and made her the ulcer police?"

Dressage: A Relaxed and Forward Ride

The foundation of dressage for the rider/horse is rhythm. I define that as a balanced combination of relaxation and forward motion. It sounds *deceptively* simple. A rider/horse cannot sacrifice forward for relaxation, or relaxation for forward. The art of riding is in negotiating the balance of the two in both the rider and the horse. Forward must be consistent; sometimes the rider relaxes the horse and sometimes the horse relaxes the rider.

One of my clients always asks for homework. At the end of the lesson I sit on the mounting block writing out exercises for the week in her notebook. Then she copies them legibly and carries the paper with her when she rides. They have made great progress.

Last week she asked for twenty ways to relax her horse. I wanted to do a more dimensional list. Cues and transitions can come in pairs—one for the rider and one for the horse. (Riding is a kind of stream of consciousness poem of movement, so bear with me, English majors.)

The ride begins with a deep breath. *And* a thought: *I love this! (horse+air=reality.)*

Give up controlling the universe—let go of adversity. *And* develop a swinging free walk.

Think about Nuno Oliveira (or another dressage genius).

And let your sit bones ask for a happy forward.

Dismiss critical thoughts—then dismiss them again. *And* be grateful for your horse's effort, reward each try generously.

"As long as he stiffens his poll, he also stiffens all of his other limbs." (E.F.Seidler) *And* ask your horse to loosen his poll. Do yourself the same favor.

Smile and breathe into the bottom corners of your lungs. *And* let him stretch his neck low as he marches forward.

Ask lightly for more forward. *And* require a response.

Practice dialing your energy up and back. *And* ask for frequent transitions.

Get your horse's attention so he can mentally relax. *And* give simple directions with a small release at every opportunity.

Think of picking up your reins, but resist for a while longer. *And* walk on.

Drop your stirrups and breathe into your knees. *And* feel the forward swing of his energetic free walk. (When you pick the stirrups up again, ride like you haven't.)

Say *good boy* or sing an insipidly cheerful song. *And* allow him trot on a long rein.

Repeat *"less is more"* often. *And* let your *horse* do the work.

Ride circles, feeling your horse's barrel. *And* ask his ribs to contract and expand with relaxation and bend on the circle.

If something goes wrong, slow down and dismiss critical thought. Feel your horse's breath with your calves, engage yourself. *And* begin again; send him forward.

Remember the very best ride of your life. *And* smile, ride just like that.

I love this! (horse+air=reality.) And warm up is done, we're ready to work!

(Because if your horse isn't happy, neither are you. Or is it the other way around?)

I Have Such Hope for This Species

Some riders are convinced that their horse has a devious plan for world domination—at their expense. Or that their horse is so lazy that any work from him will require a fight. Some riders just think their horses are stupid

"She seems kind of flighty and erratic. Doesn't have the self-respect of a yearling. I don't trust that kind of mind in a human.

It's a de-evolution to get here; riding began in a much more joyous, wonder-filled place. But when affirmative work with a horse starts to go bad, a kind of passive adversity sneaks in. Communication with the horse gives way to having an unhappy internal diatribe, focusing on what's wrong and never rewarding what's right. Riders grow louder with their cues or more critical of the horse's response. Eventually we are at war, training resistance and killing try.

"Eeouw! Does this human have needles in her sit bones? What a pain in the back!"

When emotions or impatience take the place of communication, there is a domino effect of bad behavior, usually on both sides. My favorite trainer referred to this as too much blood in your eye; riding blindly for the goal instead of working the training process in the moment.

RESET: What if the horse is telling the truth? What if you are actually asking for what your horse is giving? Or is there a chance the horse is getting conflicting cues like pulling back on a rein while asking forward with a whip?

"Forward? Back? WHAT???"

Horses get tense, confused, and resistant. Finally, most horses just shut down (by over-reacting or under-reacting).

"Can you believe the flap this human is making? She's so confused, poor thing, she's just scattered. Maybe if I ignore her, she will settle..."

Humans do have limited senses to begin with, and then our intellect distracts us from using them effectively. When human brains spin thoughts like a rat on a wheel, we lose.

"Poor Humans. They have such limitation: senses that are hardly worth mentioning, only two legs and erratic leadership skills. How have they even survived so long with such limited ability? If not for us equines, they would certainly have perished centuries ago."

I am continually amazed by horses' willingness to forgive our shortcomings and give us another chance. There is resilience enough to share if we can steady our thoughts and be as responsive as we want our horse to be.

Because when horse and rider have an actual two-way conversation, minds and bodies come together. Synchronicity! The horse relaxes into rhythm, he blows and chews, and the ride becomes effortless in a stride. It's like the horse congratulates us (rider and trainer) for getting it right.

"But sometimes I have such hope for this species. (stretch, blow...) I know that one day they will learn to communicate. (lick, lick, chew...) I believe humans are capable of so much more than some equines think possible."

Walk Detention

I've been remembering my first experience in Walk Detention. It was the dark ages and I was a training level rider on a young horse. I was so excited to ride in my first clinic with an Olympian—my enthusiasm sizzled audibly. I handed over a fat check, my horse was spit polished and I was in the arena with *A Famous Trainer*, ready for enlightenment.

My horse and I entered at a walk, fifty minutes later we left at a walk, and in between—we walked. At first it felt normal to walk, but in a few minutes, I got self-conscious. Still walking? Was I so bad?

The clinician didn't call it Walk Detention—that's my pet name for it.

Walking felt dull, like an interim gait, a means to an end. It's easy for a rider to be in a hurry to somewhere else and ignore the present. Being in Walk Detention gave me a chance to *be/here/now* with my horse. Once I got there, sadly, I had to admit it was new territory.

So I swallowed my humiliation and pried my mind open. Soon, I was mesmerized with our walking meditation. My horse was responding to every movement of my seat, in a fluid, forward way. There was a peaceful rhythm that felt like effortless perpetual motion. No rush and no drag, just flow—and both of our minds met there. I had a conscious awareness of movement and partnership that felt brand new: walk euphoria!

Awk! This gait best suited to watching paint dry was the

passageway to an alternate universe—one with better balance. *"Going slow does not prevent arriving."* —Nigerian Proverb And I felt like an idiot... The lesson ended and I dismounted and thanked the Olympic rider, humble with my expanded reality. The Olympian asked if my horse was for sale, but I was certain she felt sorry for us, so I ducked my head and left the arena.

I un-tacked, gave my horse an apologetic lunch, and shuffled back to the arena to watch the upper level riders. No one got out of the walk that day—regardless of the level of the horse or rider. My bruised ego took a small fluff from that.

In dressage we agree: the walk is the most difficult gait, it's primary and elite all at once. It's the easiest gait to mess up and the hardest one to inspire.

It's decades later, and Walk Detention is still my very favorite place to be with a horse. Even now, each ride, every lesson begins with that walk where breath, rhythm, and intention reconnect horse and rider. Because without *that* walk, there won't be *that* trot...

Learning to go slow is an acquired skill, especially with horses. All my clients reading this are smiling—they all know Walk Detention and some even ask for it; it's the miracle cure for all sorts of irregularities. The walk is the place we all fell in love, and it's the place all good things come together.

Looking for a spring riding tip? How about some time in Walk Detention, where you have no place to be but with each other.

Same Old Dressage, Brand New Eyes

I have been preparing for a clinic this weekend at Infinity Farm. It's my favorite clinic every year: Fundamentals of Dressage. One of my clients asked if it was going to be the same as last year. (*Eye roll* is this a trick question?)

Nope, the fundamentals of dressage have not changed in the last year, or the last century for that matter. Dressage is the art of riding with balance and responsiveness to produce harmony between horse and rider. Same old dressage.

Riding fads come and go but dressage principles remain constant. We might debate our perceptions about how to express certain concepts as training methods but dressage still rests on the same foundation.

Have you looked at the dressage training pyramid lately? The words are deceptively simple, but *reading* has always been easier than *riding*. It's a case of learning to walk (ride) our talk. What does change is the *experience* of dressage as the understanding of our horses and ourselves evolves.

"Dressage does not consist of demonstrating difficult movements, but of making the horse more trainable, more supple, and of giving him a better balance." Nuno Oliveira makes dressage sound simple; just a smart way to ride. He's right.

The best advice I know for helping a horse/rider in trouble is to return to the basics. Dressage fundamentals are a home base of relaxed, forward movement. It is our default safe-place to go to find our partnership again. It works every time.

Sometimes a horse/rider have settled into an angle of repose or complacency that bores both sides into being static and settled. That's a good time to go back to the fundamentals and delve deeper. The dressage tradition is to keep questioning how training can be better for the horse, so he can be better for his rider.

The truth is that there really isn't much new under the sun. And if we keep doing the things we have always done, we will keep getting the same results. Learning to approach classical concepts with new eyes and creative enthusiasm is the journey of dressage. Maybe life, too.

"All the old arts are new when discovered by each individual for the first time." from Workbooks from the Spanish Riding School.

Get Serious about Laughing

There is so much debate currently about methods of training: German vs. French, classical vs. competitive, natural horsemanship vs. anything with an English saddle. It can get adversarial.

Most people agree that finesse is better than force in horse training, but we seem to have a hard time agreeing upon a definition of what those words actually look like in technique. That starts the debate on training aids...

The more I am around horses the more I think training technique is not as important *to them* as rider attitude. Equines might prefer a horse-crazy girl to a competitive rider, or a cheerful dressage rider to a nervous trail rider. Could it be that simple?

I am not saying that a smile trains a horse. Nothing takes the place of a solid understanding of training fundamentals and horse behavior. But the best riding technique in the world won't get good work from a horse if the rider's attitude blocks it.

It makes sense that if we want a relaxed horse, we should lead by example. But riders often arrive at the barn with a busy brain, balancing stress, frustrations, financial limitations, and a powerful passion to learn and progress toward our riding goals. Of course, horses don't actually care about those things.

If you want scientific proof, I could come up with a good *Laugh in the Saddle* lecture including the biomechanics of laughter. (The act of laughing increases circulation and blood oxygenation which in turn relaxes muscles, relieves stress and stimulates endorphins producing happiness. Humor and laughter are believed to facilitate learning.) Not that horses care much for science.

Horses are pragmatic. They live in the moment. The best reason for laughing in the saddle is literal; horses like the way our seats feel on their back when we are smiling. Happy seat, happy horse.

I don't know about you but I've learned plenty from mistakes and I want to learn from laughing now. Most of us have survived tense lessons from angry instructors and I know a lighter approach gets better results for the horse and rider. I take dressage very seriously, but I do it with a sense of humor.

I was hoping that the new 2011 Dressage Intro tests would call for *Halt at X, Giggle, Salute.* Or eventually *Extended trot, laughing.* (Maybe in the future, I remain optimistic.)

I do think it's time we get as serious about laughing as we are serious about our training goals. *Seriously!*

In Praise of Amateurs

We humans are always labeling ourselves. Labels reflect politics and attitudes, or can define a purpose. The horse world is no different. We divide ourselves by breed or riding discipline. Sometimes a label is inclusive and sometimes not so much.

Some riders label themselves as recreational as opposed to competitive. This feels odd to me. I believe we do best when we ride as if it's recreational. Some us prefer a trip down center-line over a ride in the woods—but both rides have obstacles, challenges, and more in common than not.

Calling horses a hobby really amuses me. We are usually catapulted to a level of passion that colors the rest of the world a bit more beige. Amateur or pro, recreational or competitive, horses rarely allow us such a superficial stance—*hobby* is a small word for such a giant avocation.

The labels that intrigue me the most are professional and amateur. It is easy to find amateur riders who are excellent riders and trainers, but choose to focus on their own horses. There are trainers who are better at business than caring about horses.

Amateurs have the freedom to spend as much time training as they want, setting independent schedules and basking in their happy self-obsession. Professionals aren't always so lucky.

We think of a professional as someone who gets paid for the work that is done, but working with horses is an activity where the work is rarely ever finished and perceptions vary dramatically. It's pretty hard to quantify living products, and fitting an equine reality into a sound business plan is an oxymoron.

The word amateur is about more than money. The root word in amateur is the Latin word for "love" or "lover." Being an amateur is putting love above money. An amateur might have more responsibility than a professional from this stand point.

This week I have heard some complaints about people in professional positions not having the same skills that some amateurs have. We know better than to think other professions (lawyers, repairmen, dentists) put a client's situation above their own. It seems to me that it is a pretty high standard to hold a professional to; buying someone's time is easier than quantifying commitment in another person's heart. But humans are forever confusing the line between reality and fantasy where horses are concerned.

I'm sure this is a very *unprofessional* to say, but horses benefit the most when the line between amateur and professional is the thinnest.

But yield who will to their separation,
My object in living is to unite
My avocation and my vocation
As my two eyes make one in sight.
Only where love and need are one,
And the work is play for mortal stakes,
Is the deed ever really done
For heaven and the future's sakes.
—Robert Frost, *Two Tramps in Mud Time, st. 9*

Riding as an Art—Literally

I am hooked on the writings of classical trainers. It isn't that I am an elitist; it's that they use an inspiring word that I like and don't hear so much these days: ART.

"Theory instructs us that we should work from a foundation of sound principles, and these principles, rather than going against nature, must serve to perfect it with the aid of art." —François R. de la Guérinière, 1733.

Being an artist doesn't mean you're nuts and about to cut your ear off. We sometimes define art as unusual or extreme in our culture and usually with a combination of deference and separation. Artists wear black and stand apart from the crowd.

I have been a professional artist most of my life, and see it much more inclusively. Art is the most central, normal part of each of our lives—it's how we dress or eat or drive. It's something everyone participates in constantly at work and play, innately or with awareness. Art is simply our natural expression of who we are. It is pretty easy to stay inspired if art is as natural as love or breath.

An artist/rider needs knowledge of the science of horses and a fundamental understanding of the classic principles of horsemanship. But like that opening quote says, book learning doesn't make a rider. It's creativity that transforms information into a physical partnership with a particular horse. The art of riding can be as simple as the rhythm of hoof beats on a trail or as involved as a sequence of jumps or an upper level dressage test.

Most kinds of art are the result of expressing a technical knowledge with some creative individuality—true of finger painting, cancer research, or riding.

Art and science are not adversaries. Separating right brain and left brain function might help us understand how learning happens, but it should not serve to separate our assets. Maybe the best scientists are artists, and vice versa. We can start by making a whole of our various parts.

Producing art isn't easy. A masterpiece is a complex undertaking; classical study builds a stage for contemporary art but the artist still has to discover their own finesse of expression. Horse and rider have to accept each other's gifts and limitations and learn collaboration. Chaos happens, and the laws of nature can't be ignored. At some point every student of the art of riding might consider cutting off an ear in a fit of frustration, but instead stay the course.

Freedom of expression is the magic ingredient. Horses are masters of freedom and teach it well. Art doesn't flourish in a place of control and restriction but rather is the result of release and happy exploration. Art is inspiration in reality.

"Those who are bored in the arena, whether they are riding or teaching, cannot claim to have entered the temple of art, because if they had, they would forget everything else in their enthusiasm."
—Otto von Monteton, 1877

Collaborate with your horse, and ride like Van Gogh. You are creating a masterpiece of heart and beauty.

My Horse is Too Sensitive
(Part One)

"My horse is really sensitive. He isn't just a Quarter Horse, you know. He needs special handling."

When I hear something like this, I always peer around the barn to see if anyone else looks like their head is about to explode. Is she saying that any idiot can ride an *ordinary* horse, but a *sensitive* horse should be afforded special consideration?

I think calling a horse *sensitive* might be a code word for something else—a bit of an insult with a bow on top. Is being sensitive an excuse for bad behavior? Does the label imply mental fragility?

Conversely, are some horses just so dull and disinterested that they need to be talked down to, perhaps ridden with spurs and a whip just to get the point across? Or so inanely good-tempered as to be disabled from needing any real training?

On one hand, this is just a silly word game, but there is a reason it matters. We form perceptions about training according to how we perceive our horse's personality. Lots of times a slight shift of perception can resolve all sorts of training issues.

Yes, all horses are sensitive, intuitive individuals. They have acute physical awareness and long memories. Horses are frequently more aware and in the moment than their riders.

And having an innate temperament that is inconvenient, or out of balance with a particular rider, is not a horse's choice or fault. As the superior (theoretically) animal, it is up to the rider to bring conflict to a resolution.

What if we rename sensitive horses? Instead of thinking of them as reactive or unstable, let's call them honest. I think that's the real truth—some horses are just more forthcoming. They see the world as one big support group for their issue. Sure, this kind of emotional honesty is embarrassing in public, but that's why we have humility. A smart rider will embrace that horse's initial willingness to communicate as a starting place to build confidence and trust with their horse.

Some horses give the impression that they are almost sleepwalkers, preferring to keep their thoughts, insecurities, and even pain, to themselves. They are *stoic*—not less sensitive, just less emotionally demonstrative. A horse like this might appear to have more confidence on the surface, but a reluctant mentality is a lonely place for a herd animal. Rewarding a more introverted horse for being responsive is a really positive choice for these horses.

In either situation, by transcending a surface judgment that is limiting and dismissive, and *respecting* the unique individuality of each horse, we are immediately in a better position to evolve helpful, productive communication.

Respect is the ability to accept a horse at face value, and start at square one, with all things equal. Sometimes we get complacent about respect; it isn't always the primary consideration in the human world, like it is in the herd.

One more time, we humans could take a lesson.

Nope, It's Me. I'm too Sensitive (Part Two)

"You know what your problem is? You're too sensitive."
Ouch. Have you heard this? It feels like being accused of throwing like a girl. It's dismissive. This definition of *sensitive* means I'm not dependable, that I'm an emotional liability. When I was younger, hearing this would make me defensive. My mind ran like a rat on a wheel, I choked on my tongue, and my heart rate jumped. I appeared... well... too sensitive.

Whoa! Stand your ground.

Since when is being sensitive a bad thing? Granted, temper tantrums aren't anyone's best moment, but being emotionally upset is not the same thing as sensitivity. How many of us are shamed into stifling our sensitivity (and honesty) to please social conventions? Is being a sensitive rider the same as riding *like a girl*?

Sensitivity is a sign of strength in the barn. In the less-than-poetic reality of training challenges, vet calls and mortality, a sound mind and a strong constitution are requirements. There are tears, sometimes inconvenient, but they're never a reason to quit. It would be a mistake to underestimate a *sensitive* woman who works for horses.

We were all born sensitive, but there is some courage and vulnerability involved in maintaining it. Being sensitive is taking time to experience the authentic expression of life—past the surface reflection. Sensitivity is that thing that combines with intellect, and becomes perception, a horsewoman's best attribute.

Maybe it's time to answer the *too sensitive* question with direct eye contact, "You are right, I am too sensitive. Thanks for noticing. It's what makes me a good artist/mother/friend/rider. Not to mention, dogs like me…"

Come to think of it, it wasn't that long ago that women were judged too emotional and oversensitive to vote, drive, or have a voice in their destiny. Historically, there was a belief that women's brains just weren't capable of understanding world issues and were best left to domestic tasks. Most classical horsemen thought women too mentally and physically unstable to ride, except for the dullest of horses. (Unstable—there's an interesting word…) And again, a mistake to underestimate women.

Now equestrian sports are one of a tiny handful of sports where men and women compete as equals, and finish results prove we are up to the task. Women have gone from wearing riding habits in sidesaddles to wearing Olympic medals.

A sensitive rider is a good match for a sensitive horse. Do you ride like a girl? I hope we do, with sensitivity, honesty and the respect of our horses. And the next time someone suggests that you (or your horse) are too sensitive, accept the compliment.

"We don't see things as they are, we see them as we are." — Anaïs Nin

Helmet Advice from Your Horse

Tomorrow is International Helmet Awareness Day. I usually mark the day by writing about horses and helmets. Every year I read greater numbers of moving testimonials about lives saved, written by grateful survivors who live to ride another day. Courtney King-Dye is more inspirational than ever. Cute photos of kids in helmets are common. Helmet technology and design is evolving, my new one is light and comfortable. On a good day, it feels like more people are riding with helmets. Sometimes I think there is nothing more to write, but then I look around......

In Colorado, we have a youth riding group founded over forty years ago. They're quite famous, performing about fifty events a year, galloping in costume with no helmets. How is this possible? Did I mention they are kids? I can't watch a minute.

Youth riders don't always get a lot of help from the adults and Western riders seem to be coming along more slowly than other disciplines. I am not sure why; they are very bright people, as well as accomplished horsemen. What's the hold up? I know the hat carries a history and an image, but so does my top hat.

In dressage, top hats are a sign of accomplishment; you have to earn the right to wear one. Cowboy hats aren't quite the same. Any tourist driving through can buy one, along with a rubber tomahawk.

But neither hat is safe in the saddle and such a silly argument assumes that there is a debate. And there is no debate. We all know head injuries are bad. We all know horses can be dangerous. We all know someone who has been hurt. We also know that helmet wearers aren't sissies. Think Football. Hockey. Baseball. Motocross. Bike Racing. Nascar. Skiing. Any X-game (skateboard, snowboard, BMX, etc). Equestrian sports fit into this category more than that other category with: Golf. Bowling. Table Tennis. Croquet. Tiddly Winks.

Aww, geez. Now I am poking sports that don't need helmets. See, this is how the adversity begins. Again, really silly, since there is no debate about helmets and safety. It's all been said—again and again. Even the rules are changed.

I know I am preaching to the choir here, history tells me that most of my readers are confirmed helmet users. If there is a naked-headed rider reading this, encouragement to wear a helmet is the last thing you want to hear. I know, because I used to be you. I also know you won't listen to me, because you haven't listened to your loved ones already. You've made a choice and probably aren't any more open-minded about helmet wear than I am.

But I don't think that you're foolish to ride with a naked head. I think the choice is more like being willful. Some of us just don't like to surrender.

Would you be more prone to listen a horse? What would a horse say?

Do all you can to protect your family. Do all you can to survive. Injury = death.

I give to pressure. Because we are partners and being in the herd is the best place to be. You could give to the helmet pressure from your herd. It isn't losing, it's joining.

Maybe you could think of a helmet for your head the way you think of horse shoes for my hooves?

Dressage; It Rhymes with Massage

Horses have been a key part of our culture ever since they civilized us centuries ago, in everything from transportation to agriculture to art. Why do horses do it? Why do they volunteer to be with us? What is in it for them?

This is what I know about horses: They live in the moment, and don't ponder history, or care much for psycho-babble. They certainly don't wax philosophical. They like to leave that for us big brains who think too much, but frequently miss the *obvious*.

The *obvious* is what we experience watching a horse at liberty. Young horses live in the now, almost exploding with *joie de vivre*, a carefree celebration of being alive. But I see it in my decrepit grandfather horse as well. His nose sniffs the air, and his improbable legs pound the earth as he gallops off, flashing his tail. Even now, he feels a shadow of his prime, the strength and power that his muscles once held. It might be what humans envy most—that glory that a horse feels in his own body.

And that liberty is what we strive to feel in the saddle. Horses will perform through intimidation, and sadly there is no shortage of riders who bully their horses into submission, but the *joie de vivre* is sacrificed.

I know I use this quote way too often: *"For what the horse does under compulsion… is done without understanding; and there is no beauty in it either, any more than if one should whip and spur a dancer."* —Xenophon, 430 BC.

I don't know what humans did initially to deserve the

company of horses, but I do know how to show my gratitude now. I can ride in a way that encourages my horse to feel better at the end of the ride, than he did at the beginning. Think of it as a dressage massage; a ride spent warming joints and stretching muscles, acknowledging their strength and softness. Who doesn't like a leader who makes them feel good about themselves?

Dressage training always begins on a foundation of relaxed and forward movement, communicated through a rider's body to the horse. In other words, we train a horse to relax using rhythmic free walks and stretchy trots. A slow warm-up phase prepares a horse (and rider) to be responsive and free of resistance during the training segment of the ride.

If you are looking to improve the performance of your horse, the warm up is a good place to start. Veterinarians tell us it takes ten to twenty minutes for joint fluids to warm and lubricate. The synovial fluid needs heat from the friction of movement to warm and spread evenly through the joint capsule. It takes at least that long, regardless of the age of the horse.

My own joints tell me it is true for humans, too. So taking time for a gradual warm-up for our horses and ourselves is the best investment possible, not just for the quality of the training segment of the ride, but also the overall longevity of both horse and rider.

Back to my first question: Why do horses volunteer to be with us? The best reason might be because it feels good, pure and simple. A physically and emotionally positive ride creates a safe atmosphere, where a horse might volunteer a response beyond an answer by rote, and carry his rider to that place of liberty.

Breathe and relax your own self—first, last, and always. Then go slow. It's the quickest way to get anywhere with a horse.

The Dressage/Massage Warm-up

What if an arena ride had the effect of a massage for a horse? Wouldn't the rider feel great too? That's a dressage massage and this week, I"ll share a recipe for that good ride.

Phase 1: Walk on the buckle ten minutes, no contact, allowing the horse to look around and warm up the joints. No dawdling, this is a forward, swinging walk.

Phase 2: Ten minutes of stretching at the trot and canter, working 20 meter circles, with steady rhythm in transitions. Stay safe, but resist contact a while longer. Every snort or blow gets praise.

Phase 3: Take a walk break again, about five minutes, on a long rein. Remember release=reward.

Phase 4: The working phase is about twenty minutes. School at the level of your horse: Slowly pick up contact and start with transitions between gaits. Don't over-drill, give lots of walk breaks so the horse can relax and think about what he is learning.

Phase 5: Cool down and stretch from a light posting trot down to a walk on the buckle—ten minutes or so.

It's a simple recipe. I don't think it has any ingredients that you wouldn't already have in your *cooking* repertory. Actually, I borrowed the recipe from Dr. Reiner Klimke. It was his method for riding horses of any age or level and then I added some spices of my own. But that's the point; most riding sounds simple. But simple is not the same thing as easy, and sometimes following the steps doesn't get the same result for every cook using the same recipe.

"Cookery is not chemistry. It is an art. It requires instinct and taste rather than exact measurements." —Chef Marcel Boulestin. (Just like riding.) With that in mind, I'll give you a few cooking tips for your ride.

First, remember you LOVE to cook. (Okay, this is all analogy, I hate to cook, but I do love to ride.) Attitude is everything for a successful ride, give positive cues and focus on the good parts. If you get into a routine of constantly correcting, that's nagging, and you'll be a giant, but dull pain on our horse's back. So cook/ride with patience and love, nurture your horse and ride with a happy seat.

Use your timer, don't guess when it's done—in the oven or in the barn. Barn time is an altered state. Usually we lose time; we blink and hours have passed. Or we go too fast, meaning we rush ahead before our horse is fully warmed up. Go slow, literally look at a watch. Ten minutes is way longer than you think. If you ride to music, you can count songs, but *discipline slowness.* Let your horse tell you when he's ready.

Be creative. You might need to change things up. I am riding a young horse right now; she is energetic and can lose confidence on a long rein. So I negotiate with her, sometimes I need to cut the work into small bite-sized pieces so my horse can chew them thoroughly.

If it doesn't turn out, try again. If your horse needs to be bullied into work, it's time to reevaluate. Make sure he is sound, and then try a different approach. Resistance only trains resistance.

No substitutions. Forward is the answer. Balance, rhythm,

and ultimately obedience, all come from fluid, forward movement.

You are what you eat. Fast food can be fun, but a gourmet meal is art that lifts the horse/rider senses and nourishes the soul. Ride deliciously.

Victim of Love:
The In-Your-Pocket Horse

"He's an in-your-pocket sort of horse." It's a description you see in horse ads sometimes and it's probably the seller's intention to say the horse is friendly. Maybe a bit too friendly: fussy, agitated, and shoving with his nose. Or doing a body search of your pockets for treats. Why would someone advertise bad manners?

Conversely, it's a thing of beauty to see a horse standing quietly attentive to his human, with a slack lead rope. That vision of quiet confidence and relaxed, mutual respect always speaks volumes. Requiring personal space, and giving it, is the foundation of all good things for your horse: safety, civility, relaxation, and most of all, self-confidence. And since horses emulate their leadership, it's our job to raise the bar.

Being mugged by your horse is a not a sign of love, it's usually an expression of his insecurity. Tension or confusion makes your horse fidget. His rudeness makes him dangerous.

The more tense the horse is, the more we hold on; the more fussy he gets, the shorter the rope gets. The fidget/nag cycle gains momentum. Bottom line: the more we resist, the more they resist. Horses don't like confinement. Compare your tiny bird arms to your horse's neck—no chance. What are we training here?

Check the lead line—if you are holding tight by the snap,

he may be resisting that pressure more than anything else. Is a tight, inflexible hold on a lead any different than a death grip on the reins from the saddle?

More often than not what the horse is resisting is the fight; it isn't what we ask, it's *how* we ask.

But by now the tug of war is in full rage and it doesn't matter who started it. The nagging banter demeans the horse and the human. Someone has to show some positive leadership.

So let it be you—just stop pulling, pushing, moving your feet, manhandling. Just stop, let the lead slack and exhale. Let him hold his own self up and you do the same. If you must do something more, hum John Lennon's *Imagine*. When your horse has nothing to resist, he will settle. Release. Sigh. Release is saying thank you and I trust you. So don't guard the rope, give a genuine release that doesn't hold a grudge or expectation of failure.

Sure, you will probably have to ask again, and when you get that answer, give another thank you/release. At first, it's about getting a response, not how long it lasts. Patience! If your horse gets a reward for positive behavior, he will continue giving it, eventually for longer periods. He won't be perfect to start, but the shift from fighting to cooperating has started and your shared conversation has been elevated. He will choose trying over fighting, just because it's a better result for him.

When you do make a correction, be really clear. Say what you mean and mean what you say. Horses don't understand sarcasm or irony or passive aggressive whining.

"Float like a butterfly, sting like a bee." —Muhammad Ali.

Speak in his language, correct him like his Horse-Mom did. Be blunt, quick, assertive, and then be done with it. (Humans could really take a cue from mares on this one.)

In your horse's defense, be fair. If you stand close inside your horse's space, and ask him to do a task—it's a come close/go away double message. Kind of like putting a meatloaf on the coffee table and asking the dogs to go outside. Step back and give him some *space* to think, and then a reward when he makes the right choice.

Horses are such noble creatures. Training try and responsiveness is the kindest gift humans can give. In return, you will *deserve* his most precious trust. Partnerships are based in mutual respect.

"*The animals of the world exist for their own reasons. They were not made for humans any more than black people were made for white, or women created for men.*" —Alice Walker

Is My Horse Suitable for Dressage?

The 2012 Summer Olympics concluded this week. Dressage got a bit more attention than usual, partly because of Great Britain's wonderful win on home turf, and partly because of political satirist Stephen Colbert's take on the sport. Sometimes I think dressage is as misunderstood inside the horse world, as it is by the average football fan.

Still, anyone can appreciate the beauty of a Grand Prix level horse competing in his prime: the best training on an impeccably bred Warmblood, guided by a talented rider, and brought along with all the advantages.

I notice my client's horses don't all look exactly like those horses. Not all of my riders are working on piaffe. (Huh?) And no one has asked me to fly along to Europe to coach them there. Is it still dressage?

Henri L. De Bussigny was a French equitation master, living and working in US from 1872. He said,

"I have...always been criticized for not buying good and sound animals for myself, as other masters do. But to educate such an animal teaches the rider nothing. It is too easy. The master does not prove his own ability nor the practical usefulness of his art by training horses already made nearly perfect by nature. The test of his science and his utility lies in his ability to correct the natural defects of an ordinary animal and make it useful."

Yikes, a quote from someone even more cutting and blunt than me!

I doubt that it's "too easy" to ride an Olympic caliber horse, but I agree with Henri in principle. The word dressage means training, and if this method of training is all it claims to be, then the real question is how much can dressage training help midlife, off-the-track Thoroughbreds, or hot Arabians, or whatever horse you ride now.

Some dressage trainers exclude certain breeds, or excuse horses whose talent might be less obvious, but they sell dressage short in the process—as well as the horse.

Disclaimer: If your top priority is show results, you'll always do better with a horse bred for the event. I know some very quick ponies, for example, but Thoroughbreds are the breed to bet on in a horse race.

I've been fortunate to be trained by such great client horses, from rescue horses to expensive performance horses, from babies to geriatrics; everyone has something to gain, and something to give. Let's begin by agreeing that none of us are going to be Olympic competitors with our current horses. (If that changes, so much the better. It'll make for one of those tear-jerking human interest stories.)

Once we have relieved ourselves of Olympic performance anxiety and ego, let's see what good we can do, horse and rider. The promise of dressage is balance, relaxation, and strength for any horse, at any age, and in any discipline. And there is so much to be gained by wanting what you can have: a great riding horse. Sure, dressage has endless levels, and good training takes time. Maybe your horse wasn't born with uphill movement, and maybe you weren't born looking good in white breeches. Get over it.

Start by setting a goal. Add the support of a trainer, if you like. With a little focus and consistent work, you might be surprised how well your good horse might do at a local dressage show. But even if you never leave your arena, you can still have the gold-medal ride. That's the one where you say *no* to an invitation to the top spot on the podium, because it's just not worth it if you have to get off your horse.

Is your horse suitable for dressage? If he is sound enough to ride, and you can rein in your Olympic dreams, the answer is yes.

How far can you go in dressage? I'll leave that question up to you and your horse.

Cheer up! It's All Your Fault

We've all been there: Schooling our horse, asking for something, but not getting the right answer. We try one thing and then another; the work is sticky so we try a bit harder. At the same time, the horse feels a bit more resistant.

"This wasn't just plain terrible, this was fancy terrible. This was terrible with raisins in it." —Dorothy Parker.

But then your trainer gives you a suggestion and it works in an instant. Or maybe you blindly try anything and accidentally get a great response. Your horse blows, rewarding you for getting out of his way. And what looked like a war of wills is just *your* problem, because the minute you make a change, your horse is perfect. Been there?

It's the mental track that most riders run: confusion, tension, frustration, almost self-loathing, and then *ouch!*—humility. But here's the good news: humility is a springboard to improvement.

What if frustration became your cue for humor? What if when you notice your _____ (fill in the blank with canter depart, contact, bend to the right, etc.) is terrible—*with raisins in it*—and you chuckle your way past the self-loathing part entirely?

Riding well requires so much perception and awareness. We need all of our senses, including our sense of humor.

"If you lose one sense, your other senses are enhanced. That's why people with no sense of humor have an increased sense of self-importance." —George Carlin

I am pretty serious about humor and here's why: Horses are big—they challenge us, they maybe even intimidate us. Those emotions make our bodies stiff, and when we're stiff, our horses get tense. When we smile or laugh, our bodies get softer, more supple; and again, that translates to our horses. Behaviorists tell us that horses can't learn if they are afraid or tense, but most riders have learned about all they need to know from fear and frustration, too.

Every now and then it's good to be reminded that terrible, *with raisins in it,* might be a chuckle away from brilliance. Using humor as an intentional part of training doesn't make you any less serious about any aspect of riding. It just means that you have some compassion for your horse, and even more important, for yourself.

So, for everyone taking responsibility for their ride, and struggling to put a positive spin on it, keep up the good work. Humor does not trivialize the endeavor. It's the opposite—it's a very effective aid in the pursuit of your goal.

Need some inspiration? This one never gets old. I've had a tattered copy on my wall or in my tack trunk forever. I keep it handy to remind myself of the real reward in striving for a dream: No regrets.

"It is not the critic who counts, not the one who points out how the strong man stumbled or how the doer of deeds might have done them better. The credit belongs to the man in the arena, whose face is marred with sweat and dust and blood; who strives valiantly; who errs and comes short again and again; who knows the great enthusiasms and devotions, and spends himself in a worthy cause; who, if he wins, knows the triumph of high achievement; and who, if he fails, at least fails while daring greatly, so that his place shall never be with those cold and timid souls who know neither victory or defeat." —Theodore Roosevelt

Yes, dare greatly! With the help of a smile.

What's More Natural Than a Piaffe?

"Will you come over and ride our horse?" she asked. "We know he's a dressage horse, we just don't know how to cue him, but if you rode him… He does that trot in one place thing." (I already knew they bought this elderly horse from their "trainer," who tranquilized him for them to try out. That was when I asked them to refer to their "trainer" by some other name.)

"Piaffe?'" I said dubiously.

"Yes, he does it a lot," she says enthusiastically!

"Does he do it going toward the barn?" says me, not so enthused.

"Uh-Huh!"

My inner dressage queen is pretty sure it doesn't count if you don't cue it. Besides, getting happy feet towards the barn doesn't mean he's a dressage horse, or does it? Maybe one rider's barn sour is another rider's piaffe.

Back in history, when horses domesticated man, we looked at the skills horses had and tried to partner with them. They were agile and fast and strong. It seems obvious that hunting would be more successful with a horse. I think sometime around then, a horse did something like a piaffe and got rewarded for it.

When men hunted men, warhorses were trained to piaffe in battle—to keep a horse responsive and moving. Not to mention the intimidation factor for enemy foot soldiers. Centuries have passed, but piaffe has stayed. I think a few calf-roping horses do a kind of western piaffe in the box, waiting to chase. Lots of horses on the race track have a prancing step to the gate. Eventers can get happy feet anticipating the launch from the start box. And even trail horses who turn toward home are known to dance that happy jig.

Some people think dressage is unnatural work for a horse, maybe it's the weird outfits we wear. Lateral movements, flying (tempi) changes, asking for quick response: all are as natural for a horse as a piaffe—as natural as building energy and releasing it. In dressage, we ask for piaffe with the stipulation that the horse be relaxed and rhythmic, in a strong and collected frame. And that other little thing: We cue it.

On a related note: My young mare is on the mend from an injury and I have been bringing her back slowly, with a bit of lunging. Clara is home bred, not the most elite mare. She's sweetly conservative, not overtly flamboyant. And she has a confidence that doesn't give much away. But there's something simmering in her, just under the surface.

We went into the pasture to lunge one day this week, for the fun of it, and Boy Howdy, was it fun! She leaped and bucked and her hooves could barely reach the ground. She arched her neck and threw her tail up over her back. Her trot had exaggerated hang time.

I watched in awe—for a moment she wasn't my mud-rolling filly. Instead, she moved with the timeless grace and strength of a warhorse, as natural as the sun and mystically ethereal as a ghost. Then it happened: Clara's exuberant trot, high and rhythmic, just stopped covering ground. Five or six more strides bounced effortlessly on the spot, then stillness. She looked me in the eyeball—proud of sharing her secret. It was her piaffe— elegant and un-cued. *For now.*

A PSA: The Answer is Forward

In a normal week I probably suggest, chirp, cajole, beg—and sometimes yell—the word *forward* at least 3 million times. This week it's twice that, and I'm not even to my busiest lesson days yet. Sometimes I mix in some clucking noises for variety.

Not that I am complaining. Not a bit. I owe a debt myself. Every time I utter *forward*, I do it with gratitude for my past trainers who chanted it like word repetition could make it happen, bless their frustrated hearts. So I follow the time-honored tradition and pay it *forward*.

The concept of riding *forward* has some range of definition, but for today let's call it a ground covering, relaxed, and rhythmic gait.

Sounds simple enough...if you are walking... on a long rein... in a quiet arena. With each breath, there is a spreading relaxation and unity between horse and rider. Bliss: his back is lifted and strong, his poll is jello, and any resistance is a distant memory. He covers ground effortlessly! It's the *Saturday Night Fever* walk, with nearly palpable Zen.

Then some idiot (your trainer, most likely) kindly suggests that you pick up your reins (or any other transition) and your Zen is trashed by the equivalent of screeching brakes. Am I overstating it? Would your trainer think so?

And if you do find some sense of confidence about *forward* at the level you are riding, whatever level that is, then to continue to progress with your horse, that definition and experience of *forward* has to evolve to something more and better, if we can agree on what that might mean. *Forward* is an ever-evolving concept.

I understand that this is very crazy-making for a rider.

Why is *forward* so important to a horse? *Forward* is the magical ingredient that inflates circles, steadies transitions, and illustrates partnership between horse and rider. It isn't speed: it's about the balance that comes with rhythm. *Forward* turns work into play, plodding into dancing, and struggle into art.

A loss of *forward* makes work complicated and forced. It gives movements a jerky, earth-bound quality that jangles nerves and tenses the spines of both partners. This loss of *forward* is unnatural for a horse; it makes him mentally dull and can alter his gait to appear uneven.

Then, if the rider wakes up and over-corrects, her previously fluid sit-bones begin to feel like sharp rebar on the horse's back, and the harder the rider pushes, the tighter the horse gets. The more the rider micro-manages, the less freedom the horse feels. The Zen dance has become a grudge match.

When you get stuck, the answer is *forward*. Over-thinking never improves anything. With a happy seat, just *forward*.

I always feel smarter if I can find a quote that agrees with my point, so I searched for a horse quote about *forward*, but instead, I found this:

"Man maintains his balance, poise and sense of security only as he is moving forward." —Maxwell Maltz.

Funny... Horses are *exactly* the same way.

And if we keep moving *forward*, literally and figuratively, just a step at a time, in a while the riding challenges of the past are the solid foundation we dance on today. Riding doesn't get easier, but *forward* strengthens the stride and brings change. Since change is inevitable, better to embrace that opportunity and send it in a positive direction.

Riding is an analogy for life, we all know it. The world is complicated, and feeling reactive and tense is a natural response to being mired down in the muck of life. It can make you feel less than adequate to the task—but that is not true. It's just a loss of rhythm.

Ask for *forward*—with ease and lightness. Let your horse lift your heart and mind, let him carry you *forward*.

Discipline: Writing and Riding

This week I was talking to a writer/friend about how he approached a new project and he offered to share his *writing discipline*. Discipline is a word that can make a person seize up with negative anticipation; it's a punishment or correction. The visual that comes to mind for me is an angry parent dragging a little kid by the arm.

In that light, a *writing discipline* sounds like a recipe for writer's block, but it's the opposite. It's a method to develop some good habits, using positive repetition. My friend's writing discipline begins with writing fifteen hundred words a day for thirty days. Everyone seems to agree that thirty days is the magic number for an activity to become a habit.

You know where I am going with this. I always think riding and writing are practically the same thing, so this thirty day plan strikes a chord. What if you can't ride every day? This time of the year there are lots of excuses for not riding. It's dark, it's cold, my horse is woolly as a sheep, I am waiting for Santa to bring me a new saddle.

Maybe you don't plan on showing your horse. That's the worst excuse of all. We don't ride like this to impress the judge. It's done for the good of the horse. A stronger, more supple horse stays healthy longer. So if you respect your horse, love him enough to consistently ask for his best work.

And if you can't ride every day for thirty days, how about

riding differently for the next thirty rides?

Begin by redefining *discipline*. Try seeing your time in the saddle as a gift of freedom that discipline gives you. Then ride with your heart wide open for 30 rides. See what happens. Let awareness and positive perception be your riding discipline. The real story begins now. What genre: Action/adventure? Romance novel? Science fiction? Where will you find inspiration?

Then pick a main character. Choose a horse; one that looks kind of like yours. He should have a couple of flaws, you know the ones. *But so much potential!* Now for the supporting character, who do you want in the saddle? Choose someone positive and enthusiastic—and let that character be someone just like you, only better.

Pick a goal for the plot, and let it be a dream-sized goal. Even a *Black Beauty*-sized goal. Pick the one that makes you the hungriest and then cut it into little tiny bite sized pieces and arrange them in a logical progression, with room for bumps and curves.

Then start the discipline of work: Ride like it matters. Lift your expectations. Sit up and ask for your horse's best work. Of course that will require your best work, so stay positive. Perfection takes time.

This is a quote about writing, but I think it suits riding even better:

"If writing bores you, that is pretty fatal. If that is not the case, but you find that it is hard going and it just doesn't flow, well, what did you expect? It is work; art is work." —Ursula K. Le Guin

It isn't enough to meander through a series of exercises by rote, think brilliance. Ask your horse for a little more than you need, so you can give some back. Discipline yourself into an energetic version of positive ambition and ultimate patience. When he gives you a small try, praise him extravagantly. Forward! Let him know the reward of trying and achieving.

When it's time for the cool down, feel some genuine pride: You have written a new chapter and in the process, set a tendency in motion in the saddle that will make things on the ground look different. Who knows how this story will end? Maybe you'll even *ride* the Great American Novel.

Lift your eyes and inflate your lungs. This isn't a game for couch potatoes—this is *art*!

Humor Deficit Disorder: Serious Riders and Stoic Horses

"Seriously, you are no fun at all. I hate to say it, you're my human, but really, lighten up!"

Humor Deficit Disorder: It's time someone brings this condition out of the closet. Seriousness might be the biggest obstacle in the way of getting a good ride. Ever had that feeling that the harder you try, the worse it gets? You could have Humor Deficit Disorder.

It starts in a positive place: If we did a better job of riding, our horses would be happier with improved partnership and understanding. But Humor Deficit Disorder encourages over-thinking with an attitude of gravity, solemnity, and persistence. And it makes you a killjoy. Horses care about that; they get mad or they shut down. Some are stoic and hold it all in as long as they can, develop ulcers, and then get really mad or really shut down.

"Is my contact too long? Are my heels down? Should I half-halt now? Is this good enough? Will I ever learn this?" Too much mental activity will corrupt the physical rhythm. It's a disconnect if a rider converses with herself instead of her horse. And the harder she thinks, the more disconnected she becomes. It's impossible to listen to your horse if your internal chatter is deafening. Quiet that critical mind. Take a deep breath and don't be surprised if you horse does the same.

It's good to take your riding seriously, but can you do it with a light heart? What I notice about seriousness is that it seems to always be negative. Constant correction will kill *try* in a horse (also dogs, kids, and men.)

"Some people find fault like there is a reward for it." —Zig Ziglar

Some H.D.D. riders think that schooling a horse is as monotonous as a rat running on a wheel. Well, that would *not* be the horse's fault, would it? Left untreated, H.D.D. can disable a rider—resulting in rebar sit bones and vice-grip hands, with a heart to match.

Riding is not an intellectual activity. It's kinesthetic—that's the method we must use to connect with a horse. A horse might seem psychic somehow, but he is reading our physical body. To ride well, we have to learn to communicate back the same way.

Do you have Humor Deficit Disorder? Ask your horse. Is there a cure for H.D.D.? Yes. A smile will do the trick. A laugh is the strongest weapon a rider can have because humor has the power to transform negative to positive. Never underestimate the power of a laugh.

Want scientific proof? Research shows the act of laughing increases circulation and blood oxygenation which in turn relaxes muscles, relieves stress and stimulates endorphins producing happiness. Humor and laughter facilitate learning. (It's science!)

Smile, not because you are afraid your face will get stuck the other way, or because it's pretty. Smile to give your horse a soft entrance into your mind. You can't force him to good work, but you can invite him—and the most welcoming invitations come with a smile.

I spend a lot of the day standing on the ground watching horses and riders. The fast learners are always the ones who laugh at mistakes and stay positive. Strangely, they seem to enjoy their horses more too.

Here are a few suggestions from *horses* in my extended herd about how to deal with a mounted attack of Humor Deficit Disorder.

Noah says: *I never ever get tired of hearing 'Good Boy!*

Rolan says: *This is my favorite song. I love this music!*

Seri says: *Dismount and reboot. If we are too sticky, I like to relax and then start again.*

Andante says: *See me as a dynamic dressage horse, and I am.*

Jet says: *Less is more. I really like a small cue.*

Clara says: *I like transitions; I get bored easy because I'm so smart.*

Boots says: *When I get it right, I like a walk on a long rein to think about it (while looking south.)*

Scarlet says: *Please stop pulling on my mouth—I hate to fight.*

Maggie says: *Listen to my tail, my poll, my breathing and I will tell you when you get it right.*

Then Dodger says: *I'm giving you exactly what you are asking for. Perhaps YOU could evolve!*

And welcome to dressage!

Absurd Helmet Excuses

This week there was a photo of Queen Elizabeth riding at age eighty-five. Bless her heart; she has always been a lover of horses. She was wearing her usual outdoor head wear—a scarf. There was some internet banter about the missing helmet.

I notice her family members wearing helmets for polo; perhaps she falls into that category of riders who think that some equine events require helmets, but not others. It is the 'Sometimes Dangerous' argument. I used to use it myself.

But that's an absurd helmet excuse. And now I am making excuses for the Queen! It's silly because there are no excuses. The research is in and the potential danger is undeniable. Everyone agrees: the NFL, UCI, NHL, Nascar, Motocross—the professionals wear helmets. And finally the USEF, although some of us lag behind. Helmet wear has to be considered common sense at this point, right?

"Common sense is very uncommon." —Horace Greeley

The Queen gets a wry smile from me, riding at eighty-five. Old habits die hard; at this point, she isn't likely to give up riding or take up helmet wearing. And just like the Queen, lots of us don't respond well to being told what to do. I am a bit protective of her and I cringe whenever I see a rider with a naked head. If the Queen wore a helmet, I guess *I* would be more comfortable.

I think the *gold medal* absurd helmet excuse is fear of helmet hair. Really? Bad hair? Have you checked your jacket for horse dander and spit? And what's that green stuff on your boot?

Do you really think an attractive single man is going to (#1) wander into the barn and (#2) decide to not marry you because of helmet hair? *Really?* Stop making women look simple and foolish! Horsemanship is not about lounging in the barn in expensive breeches, sipping chardonnay, and having a good hair day.

If I am brought down by tough judging, then I will take my lumps and work harder. If I am brought down by helmet hair, I should get a new hobby. Like shopping.

At the risk of being called sexist for picking on women, I'll also challenge men who think their manhood is defined by a cowboy hat.

Can we just for a minute get past our own surface vanity and take some pride in what we are doing—rather than how we look doing it? Better to strap one on, ride well, and grow some character. Accomplish something you can be proud of.

People who are long-term relationship material love a helmet, so if you actually do ride horses to attract a date (?), at the very least—you will attract someone worthy of you. And at the most…you will raise *common sense* above debates about beauty and fashion. I applaud that!

And because I am an equal opportunity blame pointer—let's talk about me. I don't think I further the pro-helmet cause if I am sitting on my High Horse and judging others. It's a barn version of racial profiling. I admit it. My heart jumps into my throat when I see a kid riding without a helmet. I am not proud to admit that when I see a professional without a helmet, it changes how I think them as well. Again, my bad.

Every year the excuses for not wearing a helmet sound a bit more lame. The groundless debate continues; we are a stubborn crowd. I do wish we respected horses more, and our work with them. Mostly, I wish common sense was more common.

Why We Love Them

I had a philosophy teacher who believed that vulnerability was our greatest strength. I debated her; my shell was pretty thick back then and I had a lot to defend. When I was worn out from being tough and arrogant, I gave in. I knew she was right or I wouldn't have been so afraid of being vulnerable in the first place.

Horses are eloquent on this topic. They are the very image of power and strength, and at the same time, intelligence and intuition. In art through the ages, and still today out in the pasture, the sight of a horse gives pause, our backs straighten a bit taller, and there is a mutual look of acknowledgment. Horses are in our blood.

Do you still watch those horse movies that you've seen a dozen times, just for the scenes of the horse galloping in slow motion? Do you still tear up?

It's because horses embody so much more than muscle and bone. They evoke a full range of emotions like hope and courage and valor. They can gallop straight to you, with neck arched and tail flagged, and instantly melt to a stop—just to share your breath.

In that bold moment, we know how delicate and fragile a horse is, as well. From their first steps to the geriatric years, every day we have them with us is a kind of victory over the impossibility of their beauty and frailty.

Then it's our turn to stretch. Good horsemanship is being

vulnerable to our horses, and the more advanced we get, the more intuition we need. We have to turn off the ego (if we are smart) and grow some physical awareness of the now. We learn to speak *Horse* and then listen with compassion. If there is a problem, we know it's probably our fault, or at least our responsibility to fix, because it's the lead mare's job to look out for the herd.

And if all of that is working, we get to ride. Meaning our feet give up their firm grasp of the Earth. And if you want your horse's best work, you have to open your heart and lay down your fear.

"In riding a horse, we borrow freedom." —Helen Thompson.

Freedom sounds great, right up until we get too think-y about it. Then it's intimidating. Some of us don't thrive on air racing past our faces and we might have enough years that common sense asks us to be cautious.

Humans are often self-critical, in limiting ways, that we feel guilty about later. Left alone, we can become fairly cynical, stiff, and artless, (especially if we're over thirty). We count on the natural world to inspire us to something higher, to help us expand to our full potential.

If the beauty of a horse is the sum of his bravery and vulnerability, then sharing those qualities puts us at least fifteen hands closer to the Infinite.

In my circle of friends and clients, I know six horses who have passed since the first of the year. It's brutal; we think they were all taken too soon, even the elderly ones. Horses are heart-breakers, in beautiful and wondrous ways. It's the price we pay for sharing the ride.

In the face of such loss, a hard shell would feel like protection for what's left of a heart. Instead, remember the legions of horses that came back from the most abusive experiences imaginable and still find the courage to be vulnerable and reach out to the species that was the original cause of the pain. Can we do less?

Are you mourning a good horse? We see your courage

and commitment. Honor his legacy with bravado, and use the strength learned from your horse to stay soft and present. And when his memory fills you up to over-flowing, don't hold it in. Breath and your heart will expand as big as his. Like a rally call to a charge, let the truth stand proud: *I love horses.*

With condolences for everyone dealing with loss.

Let That Pony Run: Playtime

February is an unstable time of the year. It isn't spring and it isn't winter. There are a few fifty degree days that trick us into spring fever before the heaviest snows even come. Still, the horses are shedding, days are longer, and it's hard to not want to be outside again full-time. There's no rhythm in this bipolar month.

If the routine is erratic, why fight it? Celebrate failed intentions as art. Do something different and say it's on purpose. Make lemonade-icicles.

Why not get creative with some horseplay on the ground? Too much of the time, we focus entirely on working on our riding skills. We're so serious about work, or it's the vet or the farrier. Enough! All work and no play make you a dull partner.

For our horses, it's always about relationship, and they don't differentiate much between mounted and ground work. (Read that line twice!) They are more interested in connection and cooperation and establishing it on the ground is the first step to a great ride. Would you like to feel your horse tugging on the lead rope *toward* the arena?

The current message from my horses and my client's horses is blunt: *Let that pony run!* They have kinks they need to buck out. Cold weather creates a natural tension in their muscles—horses need to stretch out the knots. Find some safe footing, wrap his legs if you want, but let him go! Then stand and watch them in full glory as they run by and look you right in the eye, and then rocket away. Love and respect at a gallop! When he digs in and bolts, let out a big whoop so he knows you feel it, too. Horseplay!

Once the initial bit of galloping and bucking settles down, it's time for fun. Horses communicate through body language, so the quickest way to get into his head is through a conversation using your body. Start with big cues if you need them, but then get very small and as light as breath. Listen to him closely, and reward every *try*. He doesn't have to be perfect, he just has to try. Reward him and keep it light. You be interesting enough that he stays with you, even without a rope.

It's easier than it looks. Each of the rescue horses that come here from Ruby Ranch Horse Rescue start training this way, and each one does transitions off my breath the first day. It makes sense to them. So, lighten up, give a big inhale for upward transitions and exhale for downward. Then get playful. It could be free jumping or freestyle dancing, or anything thing else you imagine with "free" in the title. If you are using objects in the arena as obstacles, then it's Horse Agility, the most fun of all.

If your horse looks bored, well, that's all about you. *Too much correction and not enough direction.* Get out ahead, give him a demonstration. Crank up the music, and find an irresistible anthem, then dance till you drop. Give your horse a chance to join you, with lots of verbal reward, and laugh out loud. Engage him to follow or mimic you. It's the birth of liberty work! If people at the barn stare, all the better. They won't look at you in that bored way from now on either.

The best part of this game is that you make up the rules, the cues, everything. There is no wrong answer from the horse, just negotiation toward a goal. No one else has a better advantage from breed or riding discipline. It is a very equal playground.

If your horse is the stoic sort, it might take a couple of tries for the two of you to find a mutual game, but there's time. After all, it's February and there isn't anything better to do.

The more horses teach me about ground-play, the more I know how much we underrate the important benefits it provides both horse and rider. It is the quickest path to understanding and communication, and because it's play, it's really dynamic. Let your horse have a voice, a sense of humor. It might not be what you expect, but once they start sharing, it's hard to shut them up, and that's responsiveness.

Stay playful and keep an open eye. Let your horse surprise you.

What Does Success Look Like?

I was walking a client out of the arena and doing the end-of-lesson list. I talked about the high points of the ride and things that made a positive difference. She has a wonderful young horse who trusts her and they get better every lesson. She told me that over the years, she had never had much success and I was genuinely surprised.

It was a disclaimer of sorts; she affirmed that she wasn't a giant threat in competitions, but I could tell she loved her horses and enjoyed learning. Like a lot of us, she has worked on her riding for years. Humble and positive—it looks like success to me.

Way back when I started taking riding lessons, I was always comparing myself to other riders. I wanted to know, in some definitive way, where I fit in. To tell the truth, I am in the exact same place now that I was then: somewhere between brilliant and eating dirt. I think on any given day, we're all right about there.

We are usually our own worst judges. Sometimes the list of challenges and shortcomings is easier to see and the desire to apologize for our horse not being perfect feels like a necessity.

Maybe a good place to begin being successful is to admit we all can't all be Olympic-level riders. There, I said it. That really takes a load off. Once we let up on comparing ourselves negatively to other riders, success takes a giant stride right *toward* us.

After we forgive ourselves for our accident of birth, we should consider doing the same for our horses. Some people are forever selling and buying, looking for the perfect horse. I think most horses become perfect when we start to call them that; they certainly reflect everything bad we think of them. Why not perfection?

Sometimes we court failure by believing that if we had more money we could buy that thing we think we are lacking. If that were true, Donald Trump would be riding for us in the Olympics. Pause here; just the image of that in your head is an attitude adjustment.

Because horses are a great equalizer. You can buy the horse, and the tack and all the extras, but the one thing you can't buy is the ride. Partnership is not for sale; trust can only be given as a gift, in gratitude.

Do you want success with your horse in this year? Start simple; remember how you felt about horses way back when you started. If that feeling isn't still in your heart and all you can do is complain about money, you have my sympathy.

But if that horse-crazy girl is still there, that's success. If you can walk into the barn and feel your heart expand, that's success. If watching your horse run in turnout still takes your breath away, that's success.

"Where there is great love, there are always miracles." —Willa Cather.

Passion and a positive thought are free, and when used generously, success with your horse is an obstacle too large to avoid. See success as a tendency, more than a destination, and you are there already.

Are my standards of success too broad? Prove it.

They Love it, Even if You Do a Lousy Job

Okay, I complained about bipolar February riding weather. I suggested ground-play as a positive alternative to riding some days. (Horses tell me that ground-play is every bit as important as mounted work.)

I want to talk about another kind of ground-play; it's the itty-bitty, teeny-tiny kind of ground-play. It isn't exactly grooming and it isn't professional body work, but somewhere between.

Do you dawdle with the curry? Those new jelly curries are the equine favorite. Or maybe like me, you have more curries than brushes.

Horses appreciate a curry any time, but now especially. It's dry and they're itchy. There's old hair to shed off and new hair to grow in. It's cold at night and muscles get tight, not to mention they're all one year older. But I think horses appreciate it most of all because it's an acknowledgment of trust.

Grooming isn't something we do to please the judge, it's the first step of the ride. It's a way to practice breathing and presence with our horses on the ground, as well as give an inch by inch physical checkup. And if you do it consciously, grooming is therapeutic body work.

Want to hear the science? A curry will increase blood flow and oxygen, help reduce inflammation, and relieve swelling and discomfort in horses. It creates therapeutic warmth in the muscles. But we knew that, didn't we? We get in such a hurry to ride, or put them up right after the ride, that we rarely take the extra time.

What my horses tell me is that you can do a lousy, even half-hearted job of grooming, and they still really like it.

From the ground-play standpoint, therapeutic grooming affirms that you are a source of good and giving, that your hands can warm and ease his body. It affirms your half of the partnership in such a positive way; you are the reward—better than a sweet. He literally *feels* you are a compassionate leader.

Last year our barn had a great clinic given by a professional equine massage therapist. We spent a few hours learning about massage, hands on. Our horses had the best day ever—they highly recommend this sort of clinic. One horse was a little nervous to start, and the clinician demonstrated a very simple, non-invasive hand position. She called it *sweating* and it was simply laying a hand softly on the horse. No pressure or move-ment, just the heat within the hand, nothing more. It seemed almost insignificant, but it changed everything.

I recognized this *sweating* hand. I make a point of starting every lesson I give with this sort of hand greeting for the horse, as I verbally greet the rider. It's a conscious part of the pre-lesson join up. Sometimes I use it for nervous horses I'm working with, but mostly I do it because it feels good to me. In other words, I hadn't considered it therapeutic, so much as self-indulgent on my part.

Have you tried it? Sometimes it almost feels like a magnetic quality exists between the hand and the horse, pulling them together. It's a bit spooky; the more conscious the touch, the stronger the pull. We don't give simple *touch* the therapeutic credit it deserves.

Maybe this touch is mutually therapeutic, and that's enough. Or maybe this is how two entities can grow past the sum of their parts and synergy begins with this simple touch.

It's easy to bring to mind a hundred images of this sort of

warm and supportive touch, especially moms with babies, and elders of all species. Lots of us actually hear better if touch is part of the communication. Have you experienced that? Dogs clearly ask for touch all the time; maybe they are more blunt that the rest of us. (Down, Boy!)

Do we use touch as consciously as we could to help those around us?

In the dressage world, there is so much talk about riding position and defining the correct seat: a driving seat, a following seat, an independent seat, a balanced seat. The list is endless in the desire to give the horse the best ride possible.

I think the correct seat, the one that benefits horse and rider the most, is the seat most like this *sweating* hand. I just can't think of a polite way to say it.

Balancing Priorities

Talk is cheap in the horse world, like most places. We talk about what our horses mean to us and the goals we have. Goals can be ambitious or humble but we all have a direction we are heading, even if the goal is deceptively simple—just being happy in the saddle.

That was the easy part. Prioritizing our lives to accommodate the goal is where it gets more complicated. The first thing we notice is that horses take money! Seems sensible to make work a priority to support the horse. At the same time, work takes us away from the horse. If the truck breaks down, that might take an emergency trip to the top of the priority list, so you can get to work and then get to the horse. Unless of course, your trust fund is large enough that money is never a concern.

Most of us are challenged with prioritizing time. We all want to think our schedules are harder than anyone else's and somehow our dirty laundry is a bigger challenge than theirs. Can we just agree that we are all busy? We all work; some of us have kids, or elderly parents, or responsibilities that come with other priorities. No one I know is reclining on the sofa killing time eating bon-bons.

The hardest priority list is the emotional one. Is my desire to grow worth the discomfort of change? Is my physical body willing to do what my brain asks? And the hardest question: What do I love more than my horse? Money? Time? Fear? Complacency?

There is no wrong answer. You can be successful at any level of commitment; it really is your choice. Being an Olympic competitor isn't right for everyone. Sometimes looking at a well-fed horse in a pasture from your car has to be good enough for now.

The problems arrive when there is a lack of congruency; when our goals and how we prioritize our resources are not in alignment. Maybe lessons would help the process, but you're saving your money for a trip. Maybe you plan for a summer of horse shows, but you only made it to the barn once a week all winter.

All of a sudden our passion and joy are laced up tight with stress and expectation. We all know who bears the brunt, literally, of that drama. Horses respond to that stress immediately. They are living lie detectors for who we are and what we are thinking. They reflect our actual priority way more clearly than the words we say.

Horses require that their riders be authentic. The simple truth is that the thing we put attention on, good or bad, is the thing that grows and flourishes.

First, check your priority alignment. Do you have any priorities that aren't supportive anymore? Some of us make choices as if our parents are going to punish us later. Maybe at this age, you don't have to clean your room before you go out to play on Saturday morning. A more productive plan might be to do chores after dinner on Wednesday. Or maybe you train yourself to not make the mess in the first place.

This is where I say discipline is my best friend. It doesn't restrict me or force me to fit a mold. Discipline is raw power. *Discipline + Priority = Living the Dream.*

Mr. Dorrance says the two most important things a good horseman does is: 1. Be consistent. And 2. Change things up. I think he is right, not that it makes anything clear and simple.

The most important thing that I know about horses is that if you want more, first you must give more. No matter how much you are giving now, to continue with horses, you will be asked to find a way to give more of everything: time, money, heart, and soul. Period.

Reconsider. It isn't too late to take up gardening.

If quitting isn't an option, know that priority choices are the balancing point between frustration and happiness. Priorities need tweaking constantly, but if something isn't working, complaining rarely helps. Just change it.

Make sure your goals are your own. Don't compare your unique horse and your individual self to anyone else. Do it your way—wear jeans in a dressage saddle, use a bitless bridle, cross train with broom-ball. Find the balance in wanting what you can have, and then smile. If you aren't happy, your horse isn't happy either, so find a way to show some teeth.

"A positive attitude may not solve all your problems, but it will annoy enough people to make it worth the effort." —Herm Albright

The As-If Rule

"That horse has been beat!" is her opinion. Sometimes you can look at a horse and just tell. He's showing every sign, and he has been passed from owner to owner. Abuse is always possible, but working with him, I don't think he's literally been beaten. Who's right?

The horse is. It's my As-If Rule. His history doesn't matter that much. If he acts *as-if* he has been beaten, I believe him. It would be silly to fight with him about it. To build trust someone has to offer it first, so I'll take him at his word and begin a safe, slow training approach, and continue listening.

Sometimes a horse and rider have a misunderstanding. Maybe the rider thinks that the horse knows what she's asking him and he's refusing for no good reason! And maybe that horse is all resistance: upside down, tense, and saying in every nonverbal way that he can, "Are you nuts?!" Just stop. Continuing the same discourse (the same cue) louder and louder doesn't make it any clearer.

If you feel like the bickerfest is degenerating into a brawl, I have the answer. You may not like it: *Your horse is right.* Listen to him.

First, if you're fighting, you've lost already. Second, there's no negotiating power in being right if it makes your horse wrong. Dominance is a poor excuse for positive leadership. But if you can find common ground, like accepting where things are, you can start from a non-adversarial place and then negotiate the direction you want it to go.

Does your horse have an issue with a *thing*, like trailering, or the mounting block, or the canter depart? Horses are almost never actually afraid of the *thing*. They just know that the *thing* is the location where fight starts. They hate fighting so they resist the *thing*, then we resist, and it escalates until everyone is frustrated or mad.

The biggest part of fighting with a horse isn't even physical. Most fights are passive-aggressive mental resistance: a rider's willful temper or an obstinate grudge or even being consistently disappointed makes your horse feel *as-if* it's a death march and war is hell. Just stop fighting. Flash him a peace sign and smile.

"Nothing will end war unless the people themselves refuse to go to war." —Albert Einstein (not quoted enough in the horse world).

Instead of resisting, listen to your horse. Try a release; take a breath, and ask smaller, so that he can release easier. Cue more simply if he acts *as-if* he's confused. When he gives you a tiny bit of what you were asking, praise him generously, so the reward is bigger than the correction. Celebrate peace!

The very best thing about the As-If Rule is that it works both directions. So, if the human acts *as-if* she is a coyote, sneaking around on egg-shells, stalking the horse, the horse believes it. If the human acts *as-if* everything is difficult, adversarial, and the result is never good enough, the horse believes it. And truly, if the human acts *as-if* work is play, there's no hurry, and her horse is totally perfect, then that's what her horse believes.

Staying positive is more than a mood. It's the start of a tendency that the As-If Rule amplifies, creating a happy, responsive horse. When you feel a need to discipline something, your mood is a good place to start.

New Barn Rules

I was at a barn recently, talking to the manager about a client who would be hauling her mule in. A rider standing by wanted warning ahead; her horse (or someone riding her horse) didn't like mules. A couple of weeks later that same rider told me that my music spooked her horse. She said at first she thought it was coming from a nearby correctional facility, since it was *heavy metal* but no, it was coming from my boom box. At my age, I'll take that as a compliment. (It might have been Springsteen. He can't really be considered more than medium metal, can he?) She got me thinking about barn rules.

We all like a good list of barn rules; it's our chance to control the universe, one horse and rider at a time. I took a look at Infinity Farm's barn rules and to tell the truth, they are obvious, or feeble, or sound like something a pious hall monitor at a catholic girls' school might say. The rules are all don't-based, negative knuckle-rappers and don't inspire what I want to inspire!

Then I looked at other barn rules online and did some research. Really, it's no wonder folks don't read them. Very dull writing, describing arrogant and nitpicking barns that are welcoming to only the most boring riders. And nearly every rule has the word *responsibility* in it, like that was ever anything we could legislate.

Maybe the Golden Rule is enough. Beyond that, it's time

to breathe some life into these stodgy old rules and get a little more real.

Infinity Farm New Barn Rules.

- *Forward* is always the answer. Get happy.
- Put the welfare of your horse above other concerns.
- The helmet rule does apply to you, every single ride.
- More direction, less correction.
- Long ears welcome. All breeds and tack, welcome. (Small minds, not so much.)
- Give your very best to your horse, and expect the same in return.
- Reward often. *You* be the treat.
- Children must have adult supervision. Also true for adults behaving like children. (Of course it's always acceptable to behave like a Horse-Crazy Girl.)
- Let the music play. Let the horses dance.
- The barn should look like you love it.
- Be consistent. Change things up. (Bill Dorrance rule.)
- When the donkey brays, go scratch his ears.
- Sometimes the answer is *shut up and ride.*
- Praise more, criticize less.
- Yes, you should pick up poop. You can't expect the dogs to get all of it.
- Don't even think about smoking.
- Riders with HDD (Humor Deficit Disorder) must wait in the truck.
- *Forward* is still the answer. If it isn't working, stop pulling on his face and try again.
- Above all else, love your horse.

Fear: It's What's for Dinner

Ever been afraid of a horse? No? I don't believe you. Fear is a pretty natural response, especially if your feet can't touch the ground. It's common sense—horses are big. They have twice as many legs. Horses have a fear/flight response, and after a certain age, so do we.

If you rode as a kid, ignorance was bliss. It helped to bounce well, believe in magic, and love horses more than Christmas. Fear existed then, it just had a high-pitched, whiny voice that no one listened to.

But now gravity is not as forgiving. There are people and animals who depend on you. Maturity is a little more complicated than running your horse under a tree limb to dismount like Tarzan.

Fear is natural; what we do with our fear is the question. Some of us worship it. Some of us hide it like a selfish treasure. Some of us grow it like hay for horses. And for some of us, the fear of *not* riding is even scarier, so we make a meal of fear.

Here's my recipe: First you have to catch Fear; he likes to hide in the dark and breed more fear. Pretty soon there's a whole litter of slimy little fear-babies scurrying around. Reach around in that dark place and drag out the biggest Fear you can find. Grab him by the hind legs and hold on, he's slippery. He'll put up a fight, trying to be bigger than he is, but he's all feathers and spit. Drag him into broad daylight and smile at him, snout to snout. He looks smaller already, doesn't he? Put Fear in a crock-pot on low, and leave him in the kitchen.

Then go to the barn, and get out every curry you have. Turn on some slow music and groom your horse forever. When it's late and you finally get back home, remember that good horse-women steer clear of kitchens.

The next day, do some ground work, think Liberty, for both of you. Be the one to start trusting first; he wants less fear, too. Let your ground work swirl around the two of you like a waltz, a jitterbug, a tango. Remember that your love is bigger than fear.

"You are not working on the horse, you are working on your-self…" —Ray Hunt

When you are ready to ride, go into the kitchen and pull your cooked Fear out of the crock-pot. Put it on a pretty plate and get a sharp knife. Take a look: diminished and overcooked as my mother's gray roast. But the fear is still recognizable: gristly self-doubt, tough old hurts, dried up limitations begrudgingly agreed to. You could yell *Charge!* and call upon all your cowgirl patron saints to help you wage war.

Or you could cut off one bite-sized piece. Not the worst piece, just the first piece. Maybe you aren't comfortable out of the arena. So you take that small piece, season it with courage, and start chewing. Let Fear remind you to wear a helmet and once you're mounted and warmed up, open the gate. You don't have to ride down to the equator and back, you can walk a circle outside the arena to start. One step at a time, you don't have to be perfect. Swallow that chewed-up piece of fear, and wash it down with a sense of humor. Can you say *masticated*?

Take the next bite-sized piece; if it's tough, cut it in two and give half to a trainer to work on with you. Some days fast on the sweetness of the journey, and remember where you started. Congratulate your horse for his kind patience, and for every year over fifty that you are, score a double co-efficient. (Dres-sage words for really important.)

In no time at all, the plate is empty and a wonderful thing

happens. You don't feel full at all. As a matter of fact you have room for dessert! Pick something that's rich and sweet, thick with calories that are good for you, like trust in the eye of your horse or a partnership that holds you safe and cherished.

Eat all you want, you won't get fat... just rich and sweet.

Dressage Fundamentals, One Day at a Time.

It seems like just few weeks ago it was cold and dark; winter is miserable horse weather. It was impossible to ride some days and the best we could do was plan our summer riding goals. Now it's almost the middle of summer. How are those plans coming along?

Maybe every ride is perfect, and you and your horse are experiencing a sense of oneness and peace like never before. Maybe things have gotten a bit sticky, there's disagreement, or one of you has lost confidence. A seed of resistance started to grow so passively that it is almost unnoticeable. Until now.

Either way, if you want more or different from your horse, it's time to freshen your perspective. If you keep doing things the same way, you will get the same results, no mystery there. Go back to the basics and hear them with newborn ears.

The basics, the fundamentals of dressage, never change. They are as timeless as the dream to ride. It's the rider who has to change and find a deeper meaning and embodiment of the fundamental principles. In order for our horses to progress, we have to grow our skills and perception.

Here is what they don't tell you: *"The basic techniques, or what they call basics, are more difficult than what comes later, this is the Trap of Dressage. Correct basics are more difficult than the piaffe and passage."* —Conrad Schumacher. Oh, no wonder.

So, I'm a stickler for the basics. Fundamentals are my very favorite thing. You wouldn't think it of me; I tend to be ridiculously open minded, I have a decent sense of humor for being a Dressage Queen, and dogs like me. But there you have it; I am a Dressage Fundamentalist. I am flat out giddy about the bottom step of the Dressage Training Pyramid. It's Rhythm, the miracle cure.

The words that best define rhythm for me are *relaxed and forward*. It gets me out of my head and brings me back to my horse. Rhythm is how my horse finds his center again, too. It's how every ride starts and ends, it makes us consistent and strong. Rhythm is the best tool a rider can own.

What I like most about rhythm is how much horses like it. All things good to a horse happen with a cadence, a rhythm: relaxed gaits, grazing, chewing, and the pulse of their own heart. Anything bad for a horse, starts with a break of rhythm: head tossing, stumbling, spooking, bolting.

So step one is to restore your horse's rhythm, his relaxed forward movement. The quickest way to do that, is to do the same thing for yourself, in your over-thinking head. *Don't Worry, Be Happy*. Sing it if you need to, but breathe and just go forward, training should be as jovial as a trail ride.

Some riders think a return to the basics is a stint in detention, but nothing could be farther from the truth. Riding in rhythm is a simple concept, deceptively challenging to maintain in training, and the absolute path to advanced work.

I repeat: "*Correct basics are more difficult than the piaffe and passage.*"

Be patient and consistent. Find your rhythm, it's the horse version of one day at a time. It works on humans as well as it works on horses. Relaxed and forward is a resistance-free place, where all things are possible.

Telling Horror Stories

People love to tell horror stories. Once someone knows that I have horses, they can't resist telling me about getting bucked off, run away with, or stepped on. Somehow this incident makes them sound very cool and the horses very stupid.

I tend to defend the horses; most are pretty honest. Is it possible that when your horse tenses, you actually cue the problem behavior? Your body language says, "OMG, we're gonna die!!"and he hears you loud and clear. A lot of times, horses are totally justified, and the rider who intends to blame her horse actually ends up inadvertently bragging about her own ignorance.

Once while scribing at a dressage show, a well-known trainer came in on a very green (imported) horse, who was understandably nervous about the judge's stand. The trainer made jokes to the judge about the horse being stupid. She used harsh words and the judge laughed. Hearing that interaction has colored how I see this trainer. It's probably a good thing I'm not a judge; I might disqualify half the rides.

I hear the bad stories from new clients, but the tone is different, almost an apology. "He doesn't load in the trailer." "He pulls on the reins." "He hates to canter." Asking for help is a great time to tell the bad story for the last time.

Sometimes in a lesson, the dreaded problem, so horrible and unforgivable, goes away and the rider doesn't notice—she's too busy complaining. The truth is that most horses let go of an unwanted behavior about as quick as their riders do. Words are so powerful, and recalling a bad moment brings that experience into the present moment all over again. What if having a winning story to tell is as easy as using winning words?

"The secret of change is to focus all of your energy, not on fighting the old, but on building the new." —Socrates

Step one is to tell a better story. Words are so powerful and especially when combined with an intuitive twelve-hundred-pound animal who reflects them right back at you. "Good boy" praise when your horse is still thinking about a task can build confidence and try. If you are too stingy to say "good boy," consider taking up gardening.

At first it takes a bit of discipline, so much of our ordinary language is grounded in negativity and lack. Pick a positive set of words, let them be the rule. Keep taking deep breaths, and give your horse time to think. New story, new ending.

If you are afraid your positive affirmations will make you seem arrogant, then remember your sense of humor: "White plastic bags in a thirty-five-mph wind make my horse a bit playful." "There's opportunity for growth with our canter depart." "We had excellent forward all the way back to the barn."

If you are afraid that positive reinforcement will make you look weak, do it anyway, and praise your horse all the way to the Winner's Circle.

It is the lowest form of horsemanship to blame or ridicule your horse. When you talk trash about your horse, you betray your partnership. Always. If you do have a bad ride, it's just good manners for the rider to take responsibility. And of course, if you have a great ride, your horse gets all the credit. The people who *matter* know the truth and so does your horse.

Dog Day Dressage: Notes from Nuno

These are the dog days of summer. Initially, Romans related the hot weather to when the dog star, Sirius, was the brightest star in the sky. But we know better now. It's the time that dogs lie around like half-deflated balloons on the bare floor because the sofa is too hot, because the weight of gravity is too much to bear. I can relate.

I try to do chores before it gets to the temperature skin melts. Lesson schedules get adjusted to earlier or later to avoid the worst heat, and I'm hoping to achieve more today than just holding my head under the hose and groaning. I suddenly consider taking out-of-state clients because my truck has air conditioning.

The horses have adopted a special, even more committed, midday siesta, the traditional daytime sleep of Spain. Maybe I should take my cue from them and mix heat exhaustion with a Spanish-flavored dream of classical equestrian elegance from Nuno Olivera. Would it inspire my thoughts above complaining about the slow, thick heat?

When the prairie breeze feels like a blast furnace and I wonder if there is a form of heat-related dementia, *"Equestrian art is the perfect understanding and harmony between horse and rider."**

When it is too hot to move, much less ride, *"The secret in riding is to do few things right. The more one does, the less one succeeds. The less one does, the more one succeeds."*

On the trail or in the arena, I rally the mush trying to pass for brain cells to remember, *"To practice equestrian art is to establish a conversation on a higher level with the horse, a dialogue of courtesy and finesse".*

As the sweat, all the way from my slicked down helmet-hair to the droopy socks in my boots, smacks down my determination and sense of humor, *"The true rider feels for, and above all loves, his horse. He has worked progressively, remembering to help the horse to have stronger muscles, and to fortify its body, while at the same time developing the horse's brain and making it more sensitive."*

Working in the arena and finding out that sun block doesn't actually block sunburn anymore than it does the heat, *"Riding is a school of humility and selflessness, its practice if it is done well, tends to make better Human Beings".*

I am not sure what moisture wicking is, but I don't think it means a cloud of hot steam between my skin and my breeches, but *"Try to awaken curiosity by the tenderness of your aids."*

I have consumed liter after liter of water, am I becoming a giant blow-up pool toy? *"A horse will never tire of a rider who possesses both tact and sensitivity because he will never be pushed beyond his possibilities."*

The flies are mean, they hunt in packs, swarming and biting, actually trying to trip my horse. He begs me to napalm the whole barn. Looking on in envy as my horse takes a dirt bath after riding, to scratch his sweaty back with a roll in the sand, *"Training a horse is above all feeling and trying, according to what you feel, to help the horse and not to force him."*

Dog Day Dressage is teetering between kind, classical training principles and joining the ducks in their wading pool, maybe without even changing the water first. *"The horse is the best judge of a good rider, not the spectator. If the horse has a* *high opinion of the rider, he will let himself be guided, if not, he will resist."**

*All quotes attributed to Nuno Olivera, widely acknowledged as a master of the 'baroque' or 'classical' style of the art of dressage.

Bits: Metal on Bone

The first thing she said in her lesson was that this horse had sent her to the emergency room more often than she could count.

(I don't mean to sound self-serving, but really, you just now got around to talking with a trainer? If you're getting hurt, get some help! This is how riders become frightened and horses end up in rescue, when a little coaching from the ground could resolve the problem.)

He bolted with her all the time, she said. He was a lovely, dark gelding with some draft in him; quiet, smart, and big. He looked like an equine Labrador retriever. That soon changed.

She walked away from the mounting block with short reins and tight elbows. Mutual pulling started just a stride at a time; she closed her hands and he felt the restriction. She shortened her reins and he answered with more resistance. He tensed his poll and set his jaw, and the tug of war was on. She held fast, he couldn't breathe so he tried to push his nose out. She got visibly nervous and shortened her reins some more. The miscommunication was easy to see, and he was thinking about panicking, claustrophobic about his bit. All this in the first five minutes in the saddle. Was she inadvertently cuing him to bolt?

I asked her to lengthen her reins and she shot me a look of utter disbelief. It was a tug of war she meant to win. So I negotiated, could she slack just her inside rein, just a few strides. She dubiously gave him a fraction of an inch, and the horse gave a small blow, grateful for any relief. It was a start.

"Every aid can achieve the exact opposite of its intended effect through exaggeration and poor timing. The continual rein aid lets the horse get stuck and resistant." —Gustav von Dreyhausen.

A rein aid is only an *aid* if it helps. They started out fine, and the resistance grew on both sides one step at a time. Think about it: A massive neck on a big horse vs. tiny bird arms on the human. She's never going to out-pull him and the less oxygen that got to his brain, the harder it was for him to relax. He wasn't trying to bolt, he just needed to breathe. We are always training either resistance or release—your choice.

Maybe you are a western rider and think this doesn't apply. Maybe you ride on a long rein all the time and then when you need to help your horse, you jerk the slack out of the rein to direct him. He goes from no contact to a full assault in one stride. Is this any less painful for a horse?

Commonly at this point, we change to a more severe bit to control him better. It's like escalating a war instead of trying peace talks. When a horse resists the bit, honestly evaluate your contact. His vulnerable jaw is in your hands, and the question is more about mutual trust than control.

Good contact should feel like a long rein to the horse, more supportive than restrictive.

The secret of riding on contact is to move forward, and then release more rein than you take up, follow with your hands. If you lose forward when you pick up contact, your hands are too restrictive. It's like driving with the parking brake on and the fundamental rule applies: Ride back to front, forward!

And now is when I remind you that we don't ride with our hands, we use our bodies. Pulling on reins is natural to us humans. We are hand fixated. We use our hands to do everything, including thinking! They express our over-controlling natures. Instead, ride with your seat and legs.

If you think you don't overuse your reins, here's a test. Get a balance rein. You can buy them , or just use an old rein or piece of rope knotted into a loop. Put it around your horse's neck and start riding, using it instead of your reins. It's a sure fire way to rate your rein dependency. (Hint: Turn from the waist.)

Have you gotten complacent about bits? Bits are metal on bone. No kidding, no padding, just metal on bone, with your hand on the reins. A bit with shanks is worse. If your horse resists his bit, maybe it is time for you to improve your sensitivity and pass it on. This isn't a dictatorship, you know.

"It is a mistake to keep the horse on the bit for too long. He must be relaxed at the walk on the long rein regularly and afterwards he must be carefully put back together again." —Nuno Oliveira.

Maybe it's humans who have gotten hard in the mouth about bits.

The Feel of Forward

Forward: A good ground-covering gait that pushes from behind and feels uphill and free. Oh, so free. Sigh. We know all the words. We've all read the books, watched the videos, and taken lessons.

It's the natural way of going for a horse, and it sounds simple enough, but not necessarily that easy once you are in the saddle. So I continue chanting *forward!* more often in lessons than any other word. For one simple reason: It's about the only thing that matters. It's the very first requirement for anything we do on a horse, in any riding discipline. Forward is the pass/fail test: if we have forward everything is easy and light, and if we do not have forward, nothing works and everything is a fight. It's either high art or a grudge match.

How do we go from book knowledge or visual (I know it when I see it) awareness, to learning the perception to recognize the feel of it? How do we learn finesse? Sometimes I think the art of riding is as much about learning to feel as it is about horses.

What does *NOT forward* feel like? Sticky. Flat. Thick. Hungover. Bone-jarring. Discordant. Lead-filled. Uneven. Tense. Not forward can feel like making a long distance call, having ankle cramps, and dragging a box of rocks, all at once. Horses were never meant to move this way. It makes them weak, hollow and dead in the head. And eventually literally lame.

Forward is tarnished by the rider driving and pushing, it's a gift when volunteered and rewarded. That's why it's called the art of riding.

Okay, then how do we feel forward? Forward is a sweet combination of relaxation and swinging movement and should include a positive mental/emotional state. For both horse and rider, there is no resistance. It's best achieved in a long warm-up.

First, let your intellect rest; dismiss internal chatter. (Repeat as necessary, which means often...)

Feel your sit bones be lifted by each stride from behind, loosening your hips with each of his steps. Let him move you. The stride gets longer as he warms up, and your hips and sit bones grow more fluid. As he steps forward and his inside hind leg reaches under, your waist loosens, lungs fill, and your shoulders feel light. In this connected moment, your sit bones can ask for longer or shorter strides, and he answers without hesitation. Let your mind settle into your sit bones and breathe. Listen to his body. Set the rhythm of forward and let him carry it. Refresh the cue when needed, and generously reward his effort. Stay happy in your seat. Spend the time to let forward build from the inside out.

Feel his ribs soft and giving with your calves, folded around him like bird wings. Feel his barrel move from side to side as you follow. Let the arc get larger by pulsing your inside calf in rhythm with his stride as his barrel swings out. As his ribs release, feel him release each vertebrae forward. Ask for just a little more and then listen for his answer.

Feel his neck long in front of you, and as you turn your waist, and then your shoulders, feel his shoulders move to match you. No resistance, just flow as he covers ground softly and your body (eyes, shoulders, waist, and soft legs) lead him to bend, letting the rhythm of his stride grow. You do less and he offers more.

Feel his poll gently bend with the arc of your shoulders, feel his jaw soften and hear him lick and chew. If he blows, join him. Breathe and feel the natural roundness that is the result of a relaxed back, warmed by striding up from behind. Back to front, grow the feeling of push that has no edge; drive powered by perpetual motion. Feel each stride inform the next with energy that is fluid and strong. Bask in the sunny awareness that you have not pulled reins or kicked ribs. Let the energy of your torso expand, and feel him carry you, in trust and lightness.

Forward feels amicable, balanced, uncomplicated, harmonic, rhythmic, and of one mind. Simpatico.

Forward on a horse feels like floating on an ocean wave, gliding on ice skates, soaring on wings. It feels like being young and strong. Like he breathes into your heart and you exhale through his.

Fluid. Dynamic. Relaxed. Powerful. Effortless. Forward is the perfect marriage of Yin and Yang.

What to Do When Nothing Works

We all have those rides where the simplest thing, the thing we do all the time, becomes impossible. The horse is resisting the aid, he just won't do it. Now what? What do you do when nothing works?

First, get really mad. Swearing is preferred, and then find a stronger bit. It can be hard to find a twisted barb-wire bit sometimes, so take the grinder and cut some sharp edges into the fattest, jointed snaffle you can find. If your horse's saliva isn't a nice deep pink color, keep grinding away. And then mount up, take a death grip on the reins, and show him who's boss.

What? He won't go forward? Inconceivable! Get a whip, thrash him good. But if that wreaks havoc with his rhythm, and you know that rhythm is the very foundation of riding, then try spurs and only thrash him when he shuts down really badly. The spurs that work best have rowels with a sharp serrated edge. They're made by the folks who make that Miracle Blade knife.

Still no luck? I'm not sure... is now the time you get out your electric cattle-prod saddle pad? Or is it time to start your testosterone shots?

Snap out of it! Are you nuts? Avoid this is horrible, abusive training! There are lots of things in the world that deserve your rage, but your horse isn't one of them!

It's a crazy world in which I would even need to make that disclaimer. And yes, I'm probably preaching to the choir. I doubt you're even capable of anything close to this level of vicious riding. Still, I bet you've seen something close?

Still, most of us started riding with some version of the *Make'em Method*, hopefully not this extreme. We were taught to face the horse at the thing he's afraid of and pick a fight, escalating the fight until the horse submits. Never mind that horses have side vision and his forehead is a bit of a blind spot, make him march up and "look" at it anyway. Is our blind spot bigger than the horse's?

Here's the truth; you don't have to win every fight. Sometimes stopping the fight is a win. From that position, you can negotiate a better cue. It will get done, it will take some time, and your communication skills will benefit. In the best scenario, the rider finds a million times to say *good boy* in the process, and the horse gains confidence and pride. Best of all, there's a sweet peace a rider gets that comes from slowing time down, rather than letting time have a runaway, dragging us along. Horses love this brand of leadership.

Sometimes we have to escalate a cue to make a correction, but immediately after that, drop your cue back to small and quiet. Change the tone of the conversation, forget the grudge, and congratulate yourself on your patience. Then start over happy.

"There is one principle that should never be abandoned when training a horse, namely, that the rider must learn to control himself before he can control his horse. This is the basic, most important principle to be preserved in equitation." —Alois Podhajsky, 1965

What if you are not quite happy yet? Take a breath. And no, that isn't a figure of speech. Literally take a breath, bring air down into the very corners of your lungs and let that inhale inflate the time and space you share with your horse. Take several more deep breaths, and maybe your horse will join you. Either way, let go of frustration and ego; think of it as a human half-halt. Because your horse's behavior begins with you, a good rider should be as responsive as she wants her horse to be.

Science and common sense tell us that a horse resists from either fear or confusion, emotions that are never resolved by aggression. We are always training, both ourselves and our horses, working a tendency toward lightness and release, or the opposite, heaviness and resistance.

I'm haunted, you see, from what I didn't do. I saw something that burned my eyes this week. I was leaving a therapeutic riding center, passing a roping arena. I pulled over to use my phone next to an arena and saw such an extreme fit of horse abuse that I had to look away. The arena was full of riders—they did nothing to help the poor horse and neither did I. Shame on me.

Better Saddle Conversations

Think of riding as a conversation. The first challenge is that we don't all speak English. And it isn't only the horse I'm referring to. Humans use language, but we define words differently, and sometimes, we may not be perfectly honest, even with ourselves. (I know, hard to believe.) We might say yes when we mean no. Insecurity might create a mood swing between fainthearted and bravado. Which is real?

If it's a question between words and body language, which do you trust? Exactly, so do horses.

Rule number one: Horses are honest. They give us about what we ask for. So be clear; say what you mean, and mean what you say. If you get an ambiguous answer, listen. Assume it's an honest response and find a way to refine your request.

Riding is a physical conversation; we literally speak with our seats and listen with our bodies. The vast majority of the conversation goes on in the opposite end of the body from our brain and mouth. It isn't an advantage for us.

One of the most common mis-communications I see riders make is holding a conversation with themselves about their horse, while in the saddle. It's like talking about your horse behind his back, while he's in the room. Maybe the rider is indecisively checking her list of aids, or wondering about her position, or over-thinking the exercise. Whatever, the horse is left out of the conversation. Not fair to expect a good response now.

Riding requires awareness and responsiveness on both

sides—in present tense. It starts simply: "Walk on." Then we listen to the horse's answer: "Now?" If we don't get the answer we want, stay happy and refine the request: "Forward, yes, thank you, and bigger steps, please." Listen and respond, then go where the conversation takes you.

"To practice equestrian art is to establish a conversation on a higher level with the horse, a dialogue of courtesy and finesse." —Nuno Oliveira.

Now is where your mother's training pays off: Say *please* and *thank you*. No kidding, it makes a world of difference. Say it with your breath, or with soft hands, or chirp it right out loud. Be generous. You know the experience of a horse being as resistant as you; now train with generosity and gratitude.

Sure, you say, that's all hearts and flowers, but my horse is lazy, bored, hates to work. If your horse is shut down, it means that the conversation lost him. Around the time you thought he went deaf, you probably got loud, insistent, nagging, and frustrated. Sorry, but people with little to say frequently talk the loudest, have you noticed? Shutting down is his answer for that, too.

Do you lose your train of thought in the saddle? Do you mumble? Do you shout? Clean it up, enunciate with cheerful clarity. If you want a better conversation from him, evolve your riding vocabulary.

If communication is broken, over-correcting your horse will make it worse. You need to find a way to say *Good Boy*. That's something you can both agree on. Ask him for something small, like a long walk, or a quiet halt. Set him up to succeed, if he gives you a C minus answer, reward him like a straight A student. Huge cheer! Instead of getting his attention with a big correction, use a big reward. Attention without fear is a better answer.

Your horse goes from the limbo of not being sure what is right or wrong, to a totally affirmed answer that gives him confidence. Now his behavior tendency is beginning to change from a sullen "Whatever…" to "Yes Ma'am, happy to help!"

Now, energize your conversation skills. Talking about the weather will bore him to bits again soon. Bring up interesting subjects, be *that* person at the party. Talk transitions and releases, and forward trots that make him feel balanced and strong. Be scintillating, articulate, and the most fascinating rider in the room. Be worth his respect.

It's Different for Girls:
Body Image and Riding

What do you think when you see a horse and rider moving away from you? Do you notice that sweet S-curve in his tail? It's the sure sign of a relaxed back on a forward, soft horse. This walk speaks volumes about his rider, too. What a lovely sight.

Or do you judge just a bit, the same way you judge yourself, "Does this horse make my butt look big?" Of all of the challenges we face improving our riding skills, developing a positive body image is rarely talked about.

In my family, there's a long line of men totally comfortable sitting on the sofa scratching themselves, growing way too much ear hair, and feeling just fine about having food on their faces. And not even from the most recent meal. These same men feel well-qualified to judge cup size, cellulite, and fashion sense of any woman in their path. They do this with the confidence of men who commonly date super models. No kidding. But are you trusting your self-worth men like this?

How's your body image? *One look at me should tell you that I am totally fabulous,* said no woman ever.

Body image is a complicated topic for women. From our youngest memory, girls are rewarded for being cute and polite, rather than being strong, smart, or brave. We are held to an airbrushed cosmetic and commercial standard, and in the end, each one of us will fail. We will age, our skin will wrinkle and sag, and even being thin won't change that.

Women face a culture critical of extra pounds, extra years, or extra intellect. It's as if we should be ashamed of the space we take in this world. Some of us micro-manage our body parts, trying to find acceptance. Some of us are so self-conscious about our chests that we breathe shallow, and some of us have been holding our bellies in for so long that we can't remember how to breathe at all.

How does a polite girl, taught to keep her knees together, ever learn to ride? We would be better off to set goals for ourselves that value more important things.

In youth, it was a way I had
To do my best to please,
And change, with every passing lad,
To suit his theories.

But now I know the things I know,
And do the things I do;
And if you do not like me so,
To hell, my love, with you! —Dorothy Parker

So let's be clear here, I'm not talking about how your body actually looks, instead I'm talking about your perception of how you look. And where horsemanship is concerned, we should care about the opinion of our horse, above society. The good news is that horses judge us more kindly, and on less superficial traits than waist size or cosmetic appearance.

Here's why: We are all doing Natural Horsemanship, whether we are aware or not. As prey animals, horses survive by reading their environment, and the herd dynamic. So, horses watch us, and if our lack of physical confidence and comfort in our bodies is visible, they read us as timid or reluctant. It impacts our partnership, whether the reason behind that tension is fear of horses, or fear of judgment from humans. It could be a challenge in the show ring with an actual judge, but it relates to our internal social judgment any time we ride. Ever looked at a mirror while riding in an indoor arena?

A negative body image translates to confusing leadership to a horse. Then the more uncomfortable we feel about ourselves, the more we try to control and micro-manage our horse to be as correct and faultless as a little girl dressed for church. Oh dear, have you failed that test before as well?

To follow the movement of a horse's back, we have to let go of the stiff control of our bodies, and allow our bodies to be fluid and dance with the rhythm of the horse. Do you know this feeling? Can you allow yourself to own that shared beauty?

Try this experiment: Instead of squeezing into the corset of expectations from our judgmental culture, change your body language and image to please your horse. For ground work, cock a hip, release your shoulders, and let your belly relax. Breath deep, expand your ribs to give your generous heart room, then exhale peace. A deep breath is an act of confidence in itself. What if softness was your biggest strength?

If you don't have that body looseness right now, do an impression of someone you know who does. If that doesn't work, move like a slovenly teenager. They have this posture down.

Riding does require core strength, but too many riders confuse tension with strength.

As a riding instructor, I see tension and wonder if it's fear of the horse, or tension about the rider's self-judged negative body image on top of a horse. Not that it actually matters where the tension starts. Horses don't like tension in themselves or their riders.

If you are going to feel pressure to alter body image, at least pick a kinder judge. You can find one at the barn. When self-doubt becomes self-confidence, a supple, balanced, and confident rider emerges, and that combination will steal a horse's heart every single time. That's a win-win, at any age.

Does Your Horse Answer by Rote?

"Répétez après moi." It's what the high school French teacher said and it's what we did. We repeated words after her, and soon, we repeated canned conversations back and forth. They included lame greetings, followed by asking where the library was. It was the equivalent of a primer, very simple. We answered by rote. Not scintillating honest conversation—it got boring quickly. It wasn't long before "Merde!" crept into conversations. We laughed like we were hysterically clever, and dangerously wicked, bilingual class clowns. "Quelle fromage!"

Educators debate whether teaching test-taking skills, memorization, actually teaches kids to reason and think. I know when a horse answers by rote, it isn't the answer that I want.

When I'm meeting a client's horse, I usually begin by greeting the horse in hand, and asking him for a simple task, maybe giving me his eye or backing. I give a cue, and wait and listen. Around then the rider is thinking her horse is taking too long and flunking the test. Cue her anxiety. Now she might tell me how she cues him to back. She wants her horse to succeed and he certainly knows how to back.

On my side, I'm not so interested in him doing it fast and right, as I am who he is, and what he has to say. I hope I'm using an unknown cue. I want him engaged, actually communicating with me in real time, not by rote. I want his attention. That's where partnership begins: just past the surface.

The complaint I hear most about doing groundwork is that

it's boring. I feel that way about small talk. Exchanging chat about the weather can be pleasant, but it's superficial. At some point when you learned groundwork, there were probably three or four movements that you asked for, and rewarded. In other words, the Dick and Jane primer of groundwork. Good for a start, but if that's the book you're still reading a year later, no wonder! You should be bored. Your horse should be catatonic.

Even if you're on the right track, you'll get run over if you just sit there. —Will Rogers

The most common mounted complaint is that the horse isn't responsive. That kind of lands us back at the groundwork complaint. If you didn't have his attention on the ground, it won't show up in the saddle automatically. If your riding routine is dull and repetitive, then we aren't carrying our half of the conversation and it's no surprise your horse is bored. Some bored horses shut down and some lose confidence and get nervous. Either way, it's a failed communication.

A gentle reminder: If you are not interested in having a conversation that might reflect your horse's intelligence and personality, and as well as your own, perhaps you might prefer to ride something with an ignition.

This is the thing I am curious about: What happens when we reward our horse brightly for the same simple thing they have been doing forever? Say you ask for a simple halt on your ten-year-old, trained horse, and when he complies, you cheer loudly and positively. You're kind, but can he tell the difference between being rewarded for something he knows (answering by rote) and being rewarded for thinking and learning something new? I'm certain that if a horse, in any discipline, is capable of feeling bored, then he is also capable of feeling pride in responsiveness. For prey animals, learning is living.

Start here: Have five ways to ask for anything, and let one of them be nonverbal, just breath and intention.

Complacency really is our worst enemy. It's when we get hurt, it's when we get bored. If you want your horse to be more responsive on the ground and in the saddle, then it starts with you. You have to be as responsive as you want your horse to be. Change things up, and if you are stuck, take a clinic or call a trainer. At the very least, have a goal and a plan. Because your horse is the first one to know you are riding by rote.

It isn't that some riders have a magical sort of *special bond* with their horses. It isn't random or accidental. It's the logical result of connected work. It requires honesty, presence in the saddle. So, when you consistently ask your horse for his best work, and you ask with your best riding, then you raise the level from Dick-and-Jane simple, to something more interesting. Your horse remains mentally engaged. What that looks like from the outside is mutual respect, and that is a pretty special bond.

Individuality is the best reason to not answer by rote. People ask me if I've ever met a horse I didn't like. The truth is, once I get his eye, I always find something easy to like. There is always, even on a bad day, something to like about ourselves, too. When the best part of our horses meet the best part of us, that's when our passion gets its reward.

The Best New Year's Resolution

Horses don't make New Year's resolutions. They live forever in the present moment. Prey animals are smart that way. Humans, on the other hand, love to set a goal this time of year. The most common goal I hear from clients is a desire to build a better partnership with their horse.

That's my favorite goal, too, but I like to define it a bit more personally by adding something quantifiable. It could be perfecting a transition that's challenging, or learning a new movement or behavior. It might be tuning up communication skills specifically, so overall response from the horse improves.

So there you are on January first, with a goal and a horse. Where to start?

That's the easy part, go to the fundamental rule of dressage, you can count on it every single time. Ask for relaxed and forward movement, valuing both ingredients equally. Begin with a conscious warm up and take the time needed for you and your horse to become supple and willing.

While you are warming up, size up your goal and then hack it into tiny bits. Yes, chop it into bite-sized pieces that are easy to train and easy to reward. It will all get put together later; for now think small. This should feel liberating!

Now you are poised for the leap ahead, holding the vision and ready for excellence, but your horse is still grazing back on the planet Earth, still in the present moment. He does not share your dream yet. You have to go back and get him.

I think all good things begin with a healthy lowering of expectation. Does that sound counter intuitive? Lower expectations give us a chance to reward more quickly, and more often. Nothing builds *try* in a horse like being acknowledged with a thank you. Period.

Ask for a tiny piece of the work and wait for the answer. If he gives you even a part answer, get happy and hand out praise like it's free. Praise with the release of a rein or a lightening of the leg. Praise with an exhale and a kind word. Make praise as common as air. If you want to get more from your horse, you have to set the example.

I notice everyone likes the idea of positive training but finding patience for it is another matter. Is your brain arguing against it? I get that sometimes from clients. We want it perfect, ten times in a row, before we say *Good Boy*. Well, ick! Who wants to be your horse?

If you feel a need use more discipline, go ahead, but use the discipline on yourself. Find some patience and ask again. Go slow and give him enough time to answer. Don't do it for him. Let him figure it out himself and earn pride in doing good work. Then reward his pride!

Do you sometimes get the feeling he's thinking about it, but he's not confident he knows the answer? Reward that, prime the pump with encouragement for his intention and he will grow confidence in his effort to understand. Action follows fast after that.

Continue to visualize the best, but let your ride be a love fest. When you get to a good place, quit early. Un-tack him and dawdle through a long curry session, regaling him with stories of his best work, planting that good seed in both your minds one more time. Rest in gratitude because this is how to train generosity in your horse: It starts with you.

Expecting a result is living in the future and you have to find a connection with your horse here and now. Lower expectations get you in the habit of gratitude. It's a happier and more productive place to start.

Humans are notorious for getting bored with the present moment, we think too much and get ahead of ourselves. How do we adjust to the place where we can build partnership with our horses in the present? By starting small and take pride in the positive qualities of your horse, warts and all. Remember that *HOW* we train is more important to our horses than *WHAT* we train. In the end, it's the journey that makes the destination worthwhile.

So, here's to the best counter intuitive New Year's resolution: Let lower expectations pave the way for greater partnership and success in the New Year.

The Woman Who Cheated with Horses

I like to hear Horse Husbands whine as much as the next person. Sometimes it's almost amusing. He complains about all the time his wife is gone and the fortune she spends. We've all heard it before. It's the flip side of the football widow story. He doesn't know enough to complain about saddle pads in the washer, but again, that's the kind of guy he is.

Anyone who rides well has developed a sense of humor to get along with horses and in a social situation, most of us are good sports and bite our tongues as the husband tries to win the crowd over by making fun of her passion. Think about it. Ouch.

This happened twenty years ago and I still think about this woman at least every month.

He was the worst kind of Horse Husband, he was loud. He thought he was funny, but the jokes cut to the quick. He made fun of a trip to the vet; he said his wife acted silly. He did an impression of her using a high-pitched baby voice. He ranted that it cost way too much, and in the end, it was a big fat waste of time. He thought he was a laugh riot. Do you know a Horse Husband like this?

All of us listening who had horses knew the truth. The horse was in danger and she did the right thing. Because she was smart about getting her horse in, the vet bill, not to mention damage to the horse, was a fraction of what it would have been.

He made fun of her partner. It happened more than once and I honestly don't think he was aware of the pain it caused her. But she sold her horse. She got rid of all her riding tack and barn clothes. She told him she was done with horses. She joined a health club instead. Sometimes she stayed for two or three classes and then soaked in the hot tub afterward.

It was a lie. She moved her good horse to another barn, one with a shower. She left her riding clothes and boots there and changed before and after her ride. She opened a secret bank account. That's a lot of deception for a marriage to survive, but she was in a stressful three-way and she didn't want to give either of them up.

This Horse Husband was over-the-top obvious; some are more subtle. Maybe he asks how you are, and you answer that you fell on ice by the barn or that your shoulders hurt from stacking hay. Then he responds by suggesting you get rid of the horses. He doesn't really mean it, *probably*, but he does say it and then it hangs in the air like the smell of a dead fish. We smile and let the sentiment bead up and roll off, but it leaves a stain. And we share a little less in the future, we begin to shut down.

Or maybe your Horse Husband disapproves by omission. He just never asks about your barn life ever. No harm, no foul. Your horse becomes the ugly stepchild.

It isn't my intention to pick on Horse Husbands. Most of them are supportive, or at least not UN-supportive. They should know that a relationship that is all correction and no reward doesn't work any better on women than it does horses. They should know that if their partner is happy, the trickle down will benefit them much more than the resistance is worth. They should see it as simple math.

But in my extended circle of clients, there is usually one or two of these conflicts going on; she is reluctant to be honest about something in the barn because she fears a negative response. Maybe he is envious of her passion, but most likely he's frustrated at work or just lonely, and he vents with bad jokes. Each side gets defensive.

If you were having that sort of passive-aggressive conversation with a horse under saddle, it would look like resistance and poor communication. You could even get launched off. There has to be a cleaner way to communicate, less defensive and more honest. But what do I know; I'm not a therapist, only a horse trainer.

If I was giving advice to Horse Husbands, and *no one is asking*, I would ask them if their approach was working. Loved ones have criticized my choices for as long as I can remember. It hurt my feelings some but it never changed my mind.

The smart Horse Husbands I know are happy to see their spouse off to the barn. You don't have to love horses to know that the payback for accepting and supporting someone is much more pleasant.

And I keep thinking about the woman who cheated with horses. I wonder how it worked out. When people are different than we are, we always have a choice. I aspire to show tolerant acceptance of other's passion, with the level of Zen-like peace I see in horses and dogs, but sometimes my *humanity* gets in the way.

Walking the Walk—Literally

It starts at the mounting block. Really. If you are still proving your testosterone (yes, you heard me) by ground mounting, give your horse and his withers a break. Go to the mounting block. Do it for him.

Once you are at the mounting block, take a minute and ask his permission by acknowledging him with a scratch and a kind word. Counter balance your weight between the stirrup and his off side, and come gently into the saddle. Exhale and give him a soft stroke on his neck. Park there and scan your body for stiffness or tension. Take your time; inflate the corners of your lungs, breathe deep to your sit bones. Let gravity soften your shoulder blades down your back. Breathe all the way to your soft ankles and warm fingernails. Yes, even in January.

His walk begins with your seat. So with an inhale and maybe a light calf squeeze, ask your horse to walk on. Engage your sit bones and follow the movement of his back. Be alive—don't sit there like a cinder-block—instead, let the movement of his steps release and massage your lower back. As your back loosens, then his back can loosen more, and then the mutual massage begins. Dressage rhymes with massage for a reason.

When his top-line has relaxed, reverse to the inside: Walk a half circle and then a diagonal line back to the rail. As he walks that half circle, turn from your waist and not with the rein. His ribs expand and stretch on the outside and contract on the inside of the circle. Do another reverse and release the ribs on the other side too. Repeat.

Have you noticed I haven't mentioned picking up the reins yet? Exactly.

Walk like you have some place to be. A ground covering walk is a four-beat gait, relaxed and forward. Feel your horse's back grow supple as he steps under, and his poll and neck should nod up and down with the rhythm of the walk. From the tip of his nose to the bang of his tail, nothing but fluid swinging movement.

With just your sit bones, ask for longer steps, and say thank you. Then smaller steps with your sit bones, and again, thank you. Reward him for taking a sweet, small cue. If he only took a tiny bit of the cue, reward him even more, so that he will want to try more.

Eventually, when you finally pick up the reins, be very aware of his poll softly nodding. You must follow with your hands, by letting your elbows be elastic so that his neck is not shortened by hitting the bit. If your hands inhibit his poll, your walk will lose rhythm.

"As long as he stiffens his poll, he also stiffens all of his other limbs. We may therefore not try to address them until he has yielded in his poll." —E.F.Seidler

Do you and your horse sleep-walk? Is your walk that thing that happens briefly before and after trot or canter? Do you think the walk is for boring egghead dressage queens like me? Reconsider...

Nothing connects a horse and rider, mentally and physically, quicker than a conscious conversation at the walk. Dressage tests frequently have a double coefficient (2x score) for the walk, because it's so important *for your horse.* The walk informs all the other work. Plus, starting slow gives the synovial fluid time to loosen his joints and he is more willing to work if he has warmed up correctly.

Okay, it's true. The walk is my favorite gait. I even love Walk Detention. Bored already? Here are some walk exercises: (They should only take a few years to totally master.)

Practice *free walk* on a long rein, transition to a working walk on contact, shortening the reins without shortening his stride, and then release back to a long rein. If his poll is level or lower than his withers, it's correct for warm-up and his back is getting stronger. The walk teaches your horse to relax and stretch his back, which in turn, improves all other work.

Practice *inside leg to outside rein* on arcs and circles. Pulse your inside calf as your horse's barrel swings to the outside. Cue in rhythm with his barrel.

Walk a box: A quarter turn on the hind where there are cross-over steps in front and the hind (yours and his) remains active. Turn at your waist to engage his shoulder and use outside rein/leg aid and *no* inside rein pull.

Balance and bend improves by walking a serpentine or figure 8, with a fluid change of bend, not disturbing your horse's head as you change rein. Sometimes use a neck ring and remind yourself to ride with your body and not all hand.

All lateral movement starts at the walk. Leg-yield to start with a supple bend and rhythmic cues. If you lose forward, release and start back at the beginning.

Then crank up the music, let Sinatra croon *Dancing Cheek to Cheek*, and get lost in the walk. And truly, I can't be the only one who liked the slow dance best, could I?

Do You Ride Like Your Mother?

"Oh, Honey. You aren't going to wear *that,* are you? Could you put some lipstick on, you are so much prettier when you smile. You should skip dessert, Honey, you look heavy. Are you dating anyone... don't let him see your apartment looking this way."

That same voice on your horse sounds like this: "Pick up your lazy feet. No, don't do that! *pulls rein hard, metal on bone* Go, go, goooo! *spur, spur, spur.* I *know* you know how to do this. Why are you pulling away from me? Do it right a few more times and you can have a break. That's not good enough. Try again."

"You're not good enough." That's the message. Does it sound any better coming out of you than it did your mother? Maybe your mother was the soul of unconditional love; I hope so. Do you ever think you aren't good enough all on your own? Is that how you want your horse to see you?

Before you know it, you've become a complaining whiner who is never happy with anything, especially your horse. Is the art you want to excel at upper-level complaining? Maybe you know better than to blame your horse, so you say something like, "My horse tried hard, but I did such a bad job of riding..." When your horse feels that through you, do you think he hears the pronouns? No, he only hears "bad job."

I remember a Toni Morrison interview, back in 2000. She was saying that when her kids got home, she looked at them with a critical eye to see if their socks were up, if their hair looked okay.

Ms. Morrison said, *"You think your affection and your deep love is on display because you're caring for them. It's not. When they see you, they see the critical face. But if you let your face speak what's in your heart...because when they walked in the room, I was glad to see them. It's just as small as that, you see."*

I've remembered this interview for so long because it illuminated the choice. Both statements were true: the external surface of messy hair and the love she felt internally, in her heart. She chose the tone of her *Mother Voice*.

Ms. Morrison says it's a small change to show your heart instead of your critical eye. To me it's more of an acquired skill. It's not about how much we love horses or our commitment to riding. The truth is a lot of us were taught to see what was wrong because it's an easier, cheaper way to seem smart. It is always easier to find fault than it is to affirm what's good.

It's pretty common for a client (trainer, vet, farrier) to give me the eyebrow squint for rewarding a horse with a *good boy* before he has done anything. When did we get so stingy with encouragement? What is the resistance to encouraging *try* instead of standing back doubting?

Do you think being positive is acceptable for a trail horse, but not a performance horse? Is it okay for a lower level dressage horse, but do upper level movements require more enforcement because the work is harder? No. No again. If you want your horse to advance in training, you have to advance as a rider. Some of that is technique and some of it is becoming better at training positive confidence in both of you.

In defense of women, we generally aren't that good at receiving compliments. Sometimes it's easier to hear we're wrong than to accept praise, for our horse or ourselves. We deflect with a joke or awkwardness. We are self-effacing to the point of dysfunction. When did confidence become as elusive as thigh gap?

The seed that grows is the one we water, and the choice is yours. Reward the good, and for now, ignore the rest. Start with, "I'm a good rider!" Did anyone believe you?

You have a default riding position: Heels down, centered in the saddle, shoulders relaxed. Do you have a default mental position? I encourage my clients to have a riding mantra. Make it up, something meaningful to you. Something that expresses how your heart feels when you see your horse. (If you heart doesn't light up there's still time to take up stamp collecting.)

I've used the same mantra every ride for over twenty-five years and it's inanely simple: *I love my horse.* I say it even if I'm on your horse. As soon as my seat lands in the saddle, I take a deep breath and say it. I say it every time I halt at X to begin a dressage test and every time things start to come apart. I say it twice if I'm working with a rescue.

I say what's in my heart before the first stride partly because there is still a horse-crazy girl inside me, and partly because I am a professional and I've proven to myself time and again that it *always* gets better results.

If it's hard for you to say, if your voice sounds tiny, choose a different *Mother Voice,* one filled with loud love. And maybe the Big Boss Mare in the Sky will chime in with, "Good Girl. Nice job, ride on!"

Bad Timing Explained

Most of us read the training books and do the best we can to apply them in the saddle. We all think we define those words the same way, but we don't all get great results.

Maybe you aren't a flawless rider but you're not a total disaster in the saddle either. If you are in the immense gray area of riders in the middle and trying to do better, consider this: A small adjustment in timing can make a huge difference. There's an instant where a horse and human partnership becomes adversarial, and I want to magnify that instant big enough to recognize, so you can have a do-over. Humor me, this gets a little fussy on paper.

Say your horse doesn't want to go forward (or whatever). You know enough to ask small first and then slowly escalate if the horse doesn't respond. You're ready—as the leader—to enforce the horse's expected lazy response. Since he isn't going forward now, you're prepared to judge and correct, even before the first request. When you actually ask for more forward, the process goes something like this: (visualize this in your head using a pointer and a stick figure of a horse and rider, please.) The idea appears in your brain, it travels down your spine to your seat and on to your legs or feet. Eventually your horse feels the sensation and that information travels through his body to his spine and up his neck to his brain, he ponders it for a brief moment and suddenly, even rudely...

Whack! Time's up, pencils down, time for a spanking!

Did you give him enough time? Is it possible that you interrupted him just as he was preparing to go? Maybe in the same instant he was answering, you judged him as disobedient and escalated the cue, with more leg or maybe a tap with the whip. (This is the important instant!) If the timing is off, it can feel to the horse like he just got punished for trying. If the correction was too fast or hard, he wonders if the first cue was not a cue for forward, but instead a warning that a correction was on the way. Then instead of going forward at the first cue, he's learned to anticipate the wrong thing.

Next the rider prepares for an even bigger cue. This is going to need strength (we think), and maybe he will resist more, so the seat stops following and the legs grab on (the cue for a half halt, if not a full halt) and the reins get tight because that's what the rest of the body did. Lots of horses consider set hands that don't follow the exact same thing as pulling back on the reins. You can disagree but he's actually the one who gets to judge this part. Now the leg kicks hard enough to bruise a rib. It's a conflicting message, legs say *Forward* but seat and hands say *Don't you dare.*

Here's the problem: Your brain is spinning for obedience so you don't notice how much the rest of your body is working against it. You've seen other riders do this, haven't you?

And by the way, as you have been thinking in your head about what to do, and he's been trying to respond somehow in his confusion, your partnership has become adversarial. Frustrated. And now both of you are thinking *Whatever I do is wrong*! Have three minutes passed since the first ask for forward? How's the ride going so far?

Here's the do-over: Rewind back to the first ask for forward. You asked lightly and while the message is traveling back and forth, you breathe. Give him the benefit of the doubt and just as you are ready to escalate the first time, be patient and take one more deep breath. He will most likely go on that inhale. If he gives you a tiny half-stride more forward, praise him for doing what you asked. Then repeat. When his try is rewarded, he learns in hindsight that he has done the right thing, and that builds confidence. Literally. No one is in a defensive mode and both of you are at *Whatever I do is right!* (Or at least headed that way.)

They say the definition of insanity is doing the same thing over and over and expecting a different result. It follows that if your horse needs improvement, it has to start with you. For a rider that means improving your perception in the saddle and illuminating the dark little corners of communication. The training conversation has to go deeper than the surface perception.

Does this method seem slow? Should a leader demand more, better, faster? It's absolutely true we want our horses to be more responsive, but that's trained differently. It's lots of walk-trot transitions that pave the path to enlightenment! In the beginning of the ride, the transitions won't be perfect. Say thanks and ask again. Tune him up by rewarding the good, that's a far different intention than correcting.

Horses and riders are always working on a tendency toward partnership but we even define that differently. Do you want dominance or responsiveness? Seriously, they are not the same thing. The reason this instant in the timing of a cue matters so very much, is that it's the moment when you let your horse know who you really are.

Your Horse Has Ulcers

I don't usually say it that bluntly but I wanted to get your attention. I need to make a payment on a debt. Usually I start with the term *sour stomach*. No one likes to hear *ulcers* because it opens the flood gates of guilt, blame, and angst. Not to mention the check book. But that's about us, can we talk horse? May I explain my thinking?

First: Horses were never designed to live at our convenience. They have a prickly digestive system that runs best on grazing 24/7 in nice green pastures. Frankly, they weren't designed to be ridden either. Big bodies on small feet, and the task of balancing a rider on their back is a big physical challenge to them—something we humans love to underestimate.

Horses have another huge weakness. They are all very sensitive. We like to think some horses are more sensitive than others, but each individual horse feels stress and responds differently. Some will shut down while others wear their feelings on their sleeves and over-react, but make no mistake. All horses are sensitive victims of stress and worry. Ironically these same qualities of sensitivity make them capable of immense understanding and partnership—meaning this "weakness" is something we love about them.

Counter-balance against all those negatives—and a few dozen more too complex or long-winded to list here—this one princely gift: Horses volunteer. It defies common sense, but horses (and dogs) choose to be with us. I'm sceptical that men domesticated them; I think it happened the other way around.

When horses lay their precious gift of trust freely, prey to predator, into our hands, we owe it to them to do our very best. For all the ways horses lift us and carry us through life, we owe a debt. For the time it was within his right to buck us off and not look back, but instead he was patient, we owe a debt. And most of all, for the simple joy of being with an animal of such strength, beauty and intellect, we owe a debt. If horses don't take your breath away every day, then you're doing it wrong.

I think by now we have all heard the ulcer statistics: ninety-three percent of horses on the track, sixty percent of performance horses, over fifty-seven percent of foals during weaning, the list goes on. The chances are that at some point in most horse's lives, ulcers were there. With these numbers, why do we resist the possibility instead of embrace the chance to help them?

Here is the statistic that we should be the most concerned about: Of the horses scoped and diagnosed with ulcers, fifty percent showed no symptoms—silent ulcers. There's a well-documented connection between ulcers and colic, the leading cause of premature equine death.

If a horse is struggling with behaviors we don't like, it should always the first step to rule out health issues, and I am not sure, short of a costly diagnosis, that we can ever rule out ulcers conclusively. Sometimes horses communicate pain but we hear it as bad behavior instead. While we should never condone bad behavior, how else do they have to get our attention when pain persists?

In the face of these numbers, as a trainer I would rather err on the side of caution. More than that, since people frequently hire trainers when they run into problems with their horses, I think trainers have a responsibility to be especially knowledgeable about ulcers. The first "diagnosis" might be a suggestion from us.

Am I some sort of wing nut who thinks all horses should

be returned to nature? Nope, my Grandfather Horse would be dead in a day. Does this mean that every horse needs a $1000 course of prescribed medication? Nope. The goal is to save horses *and* money with some information that too many of us take for granted.

Horse owners do need to educate themselves. There is so much good information available EGUS/ulcer symptoms and care, and it should be required knowledge, just like hoof care or first-aid. Good horsemanship always means putting your horse's well-being above your personal convenience.

Secondly, we need to manage their care as naturally as possible. Free choice hay is a good start. Skipping sweet feed is close behind. If your horse needs some extra help, the market for supplements has quadrupled in the last few years. Many are inexpensive and there are lots of holistic products.

Finally, who knows your horse better than you? Horse owners are always looking to improve communication and partnership with their horses. If that is going to happen, we have to listen to them, even when they tell us something we don't want to hear.

I had a young horse who was very food aggressive but instead of listening to him, I trained the behavior out of him. The ulcers got worse, but he was more polite when I fed him. I'm still apologizing. Even the best training cannot heal a medical condition; those are two separate things. He taught me to listen all horses better, and I owe him a huge debt.

Do you have a gelding who makes faces or sticks his tongue out? Or a mare who is always pinning her ears? Are they physically anxious or uncomfortable? Or maybe just not the happy, willing horse you remember? Respect your horse: listen closely and don't let his behavior distract you from his message. You owe him the benefit of the doubt.

Explaining Dressage: the Small Print

First of all, the reason dressage needs some explaining is that the there are some misconceptions about this riding discipline. Some people think that dressage is a hyper-correct, micro-managed, soul-killing, brain-numbing, and sit-bone-driving sport with all the drama and thrill of curling. But with less cool outfits. The Norwegian curling pants are world famous. It kills me to admit it, but these boys do seem like thrill seekers, comparatively speaking.

Other people think that dressage is a bliss-ninny riding discipline that uses yoga breathing and astral projection to create just the perfect vibration of molecules when alternate calf muscles flex and release in rhythm the horse's rib cage and then, if the horse is a Taurus and the rider is a Virgo, and the moon is waxing, and there are four ounces more weight in the outside sit bone, a light canter depart is inevitable.

And these differences of opinion come from *inside* the dressage world. Who knows what jumpers or ropers or trail riders think?

There is something we like to say when we see people with an irrational fear of white breeches or paranoia that we will put two bits in their horse's mouth. We make it simple: "Dressage is a French word that means training," (See fine print below.) "That's all." The rider exhales and is visibly relieved. How hard can that be? (*Muffled laughter*)

Dressage is a classical curriculum of training that encourages a horse become strong, supple, and responsive to cues. It begins with the horse and rider moving rhythmically in a relaxed, ground covering gait. I could write another twenty thousand pages describing dressage, but I will spare you that, if we can just assume good intention and go with this brief description.

I'm an equine professional, meaning that sometimes I train the horse and sometimes the rider, but my favorite is to train a horse/rider. More inclusive that way. When a rider hires me, they introduce themselves by telling me they have a great horse and then list his problems. He's lazy, or spooky, or disobedient. Worst, sometimes people say their horse has gone about as far as he can, or they've outgrown their horse and have to move on.

Just an opinion, but unless you have a Shetland pony and you just had a wild growth spurt between eighth and ninth grade, you haven't outgrown anything. It is possible that you have reached the end of your training grasp. Listening with trainer's ears to a horse's problems usually says something about the rider, too.

Right now, your horse goes the way he does because that's how you're riding him. If you want him to improve, riding differently comes first. In other words, maybe you don't outgrow him so much as you reach the top of your communication and riding skill. You don't actually know if he can go farther or not, because you don't know how to ask him to go farther. (Your horse is grateful to hear this part.)

(Small Print at Bottom of Page.) *Yes, dressage means training, but although we imply that it's the horse who gets trained, strictly speaking, that is less than honest. Or maybe more precisely, it's just not true. It's the rider who gets trained.*

If you are thinking that your horse isn't up to the task this year, or that it's time to find a partner with more skill, or even if you are thinking you want to start a new horse instead of finishing the one you have, please reconsider. The rub of ambition you feel could inspire a leap forward in your riding skill and perception. Maybe instead of asking what level your horse is, we should ask what level the rider is. And not just in dressage, but any riding discipline. I've seen some upper level trail horses whose riders were inspiring.

"... *I should like to remind every rider to look to himself for the fault whenever he has any difficulties with his horse.*" —Alois Podhajsky, who is blunt. Maybe the quick cut is less painful, but he's right.

A student of the art of riding has to acquire enough good-natured humility to diffuse self-blame, while mustering the confidence to try again. Dressage riders see themselves as students of the horse forever. Several Dressage Masters have said old age was exciting because after decades in the saddle, they were finally starting to learn to ride.

If you're thinking of investing this spring, maybe the investment in yourself will yield the best return. This is my advice: Hire a good trainer. This stuff is hard to learn from books and videos that don't have eyes and can't actually see what your horse/rider is doing. If it truly is time for a different horse, all the more reason to invest in yourself as well.

The Art is in the Transition

When I see kids learning to drive these days in compact cars with automatic transmissions, I wonder *where's the challenge?* Back in my day (beware when a gray-haired woman begins a sentence this way), we didn't have medicated driving instructors and signs on the car warning others that there was a student driver (hysteric child) behind the wheel.

I learned to drive on the Washington state beach, in a big American car with a manual transmission and my father yelling profanity. He didn't give me any pointers, just lots of criticism. And remember how the clutch had that death-defying ability to create a multi-whiplash experience before you even got to five mph? A little like a carnival ride actually. My father was not the sort to go on a carnival ride. The driving lesson came to an abrupt halt when I hit a whale carcass. Yes, it was very visible. In my defense, my father wanted to see what it was and from a distance it was hard to identify. And I didn't hit it hard, just bumped it really. I was almost stopped. The carcass did smell pretty ripe and some of it got hung up on the bumper. I walked back to where we were staying.

A more hormonal teenage girl would have burst into tears and settled for the family station wagon, but not me. I was born for cross-country trips in a Volkswagen bug. I had to master the shift. A year later, my boyfriend tried to teach me; he didn't yell profanity, he was the tense silent type.

In the end, I *borrowed* my boyfriend's car at three a.m. one morning, and splatted and jolted my way to the mall. After three hours of touring the lot, and without the external male distraction, I learned to shift smoothly, lightly, powerfully. And back in reverse.

This is how the Urban Dictionary describes *clutch*: the crucial moment that comes between winning and losing (derived from the clutch mechanism in a manual car, where perfect timing can mean the difference between a launch and a stall). Is this a great analogy for riding or what?

Horses don't come in a choice of automatic or manual transmission, but we can ride them that way. In other words, most anyone can get a trot. The telling part is the first few strides going into or coming out of each gait. Is the horse relaxed and balanced or do the gears grind? Are you a *no pointers and just lots of criticism* sort like my father? Does your horse respond like a teenage girl? (*Whatever!*)

The ART is in the transition—that ease of shifting between gaits is where partnership exists—jerky and unbalanced or smooth and powerful.

We all know a bad transition when we see one: A jarring loss of balance, a human with jerky hands, tight legs and a bouncing seat, cuing a horse to have a tense poll, hollow neck and back, and irregular strides. Usually because the cue is too big, too quick, or too harsh. In other words, you and your horse are in the car with me and my father and you don't want to be there either.

The ideal transition should feel like a jet taking off or landing: A forward push from behind with each stride balanced and level, with a rhythmic and gradual increase or decrease in gait. The transition between gaits isn't trotting so fast that the horse is forced to canter (like the roar of driving a car at forty-five mph in second gear) but a change of gait so the horse can cover more ground, relaxed and with less strength (like engaging the clutch and going into a higher gear so the engine can work less.)

Disclaimer: Riding, being a physical interactive conversation with another sentient being who weighs a thousand pounds, is hard to learn from the written page. There is no shortage of techniques described but since we don't all use words the same way, it's virtually impossible to tell if you have it right without a ground person. I'm going to describe how it could *feel* in hopes of inspiring better technique. Did that make sense?

Upward transitions begin with an inhale, the lungs expand and we are a bit lighter in the saddle. There is energy in our core and the horse begins to respond. Apply both calves, inhale again, give a verbal command if you like, and then give the horse time to respond. If you get even a small response, reward him and ask for more. Slow and steady, the jet builds speed until it leaves the ground and flies. Note: If you go to the whip before he has time to answer, he will shut down. If you nag every stride with your legs he will be dull to the constant assault. You think he's lazy and needs spurs, but your cues are so hidden in trash that he can't find them. Stay with your horse; let the rhythm build stride by stride. You maintain neutral balance and stay out of his way, so he can do the same. Forward, the joyous call to partnership, forward!

Note: The rider isn't the one who trots or canters. We just give the cue and then the horse does the work. It seems obvious in print, but all of us have seen people who over-ride their horse off his feet and out of balance.

Downward transitions begin with an exhale and we are a bit softer in the saddle. Like a jet landing, shoulders stay back for balance and there is a gradual stride-by-stride slowing. Half-halt as much as you need, reward him for the tiniest response so he knows he got it right and he is confident to try harder, and then cue the new gait. Melt softly into the saddle, don't collapse and wreck. Relax and exhale again. Core tension is not the same thing as core strength. Stay inside of each stride, connected with your seat. If you are cuing his *body* to decelerate, use your *body* to cue it. It's not a job for your hands; pulling the bit creates tension and resistance.

In riding a dressage test, we score each transition. When does it begin? In the first score box of Training Level, Test 1, the directives include *Balanced Transition.* Scoring transitions continues through Grand Prix. I love how these tests are designed. If you ride them correctly, whether you compete or not, the result is a strong, supple and responsive horse. Because we don't ride this way to please the judge, we do it for the good of the horse. Yay, dressage!

Subtle Abuse:
When Aids Become Weapons

My client's mare is lovely; a very well-bred athletic horse. When my client bought her, the previous owner suggested my client get a cowboy to ride her at first, she needed spurs all the time and the horse was *"mare-y"*, whatever that means. I get a little *mare-y* myself at the suggestions.

My client decided the best course of action was working on the fundamentals. That's where I came in. My initial feeling was that the young mare was pushed hard and fast. She needed some decompress time and although she looked for the familiar spur pain, we took a slow approach to give her time to notice the fighting had stopped.

The mare was absolutely terrified of plastic bags, oddly, because it was an out-of-context fear compared to her wonderful, smart personality in general. She was not at all spooky.

One day my client sent me to the breeder's website and I watched several videos of them with young horses. In each video, the humans were aggressively stepping forward, viciously flapping bags at the weanling's eyes. I got squinty just watching. The young horses were confused more than obedient, and some were truly frightened. The breeders seemed to have no awareness of the response, never gave a release, and of course, there was no reward. It's just bad horsemanship.

In a way, these sale videos showed fearful rescue horses.

Worst of all, I saw what my client saw. The impact of this early work had infected the whole training process. Was this where her defensiveness began? Sure looked like it to me.

No, I don't think plastic bags are cruel. They are just bags, for crying out loud. There is no innate wickedness in spurs or whips, or the biggest one for me, bits. This topic is in response to a request from a reader. These are her words:

"I'm not talking about clear and extreme cases of abuse, but rather more subtle cases. Perhaps ones where there are no visible wounds or scars, but the methods used are confusing, unfair, and do not take into account how horses learn. For example, when amateur owner with a 'stubborn or challenging' horse meets inexperienced trainer. I add quotes because I believe often the horse is just confused or frustrated. I've seen cases where horses were hit over and over for no reason—no disobedience occurred—for the purpose of 'desensitizing' or 'teaching' it that the owner could hit it whenever they wanted and the horse had to accept it."

It's a long quote, but I don't think I can say it better. Most of us have seen the same thing.

When we don't get the response we want, rather than checking fundamentals and tuning up the rider's ask and the horse's response, we "get a bigger gun." More whip, spurs, a stronger bit. If a little is good, more is better. This is not just a bad idea, it's dead wrong.

It starts with good intention, perhaps coupled with a video recently watched. (A reminder here, not everyone who is famous for videos is necessarily any good with horses.) On top of this, some of us were born with body perception, those of us who were dancers or athletes, but the rest of us don't always know what our hands are doing way down there at the end of our arms. Our brains get attached to the technique we are attempting, we get frustrated we're losing forward so we get a little louder, and by this I mean harder with our aids. Then we are still stuck in our heads thinking about obedience to our aids, and… and…

Oh, yeah, the horse. Maybe he is over-reacting or maybe he is shut down, but in either case you are just now noticing his answer. There has been so much focus on using the aid, there was no listening to the horse.

People love to complain that with the internet and smartphones people aren't spending enough literal face time with family and friends. I feel that exact way about training aids. An inanimate training aid never replace an actual conversation where both sides try to understand each other.

If your aid isn't working and you think you need something stronger, try less. When your horse doesn't understand, yelling the same thing louder isn't the solution. Find a way to communicate more clearly, use rewards to let the horse know they are getting warmer, closer to the right answer. Remember: Riding is an art, you need creativity. Lighten up, physically and mentally!

No joke, *whisper the cue*. Use a calf instead of a spur, or release the reins and ask. Use more brain and less brawn.

"Every aid can achieve the exact opposite of its intended effect through exaggeration and poor timing. The continual rein aid lets the horse get stuck and resistant. The poorly timed or rough driving calf can bring disorder into the legs, the gait. The seat that drives too long and too intensively makes the horse roll away on the forehand." —Gustav von Dreyhausen, mid-1800's.

Less is more: It's the one thing horses are forever trying to teach humans, the one thing that we just don't trust. Flies know that a light, somewhat irritating, cue is plenty to move a horse but humans can be such slow learners.

A Recipe for Patience

I want to start by saying I used to consider patience the exact same thing as procrastination. I had no time for patience. It was a dull, slow-witted thing, so foreign to me that I couldn't even figure out what it was that people did while they were being patient. You know? Patience isn't even a verb. Trying to be patient stressed me out.

My parents gave up early, having no patience with my impatience. The usual public school education didn't even touch it. Clearly I needed horses to teach me.

Now I've been at it long enough to have had several horses school me and I have hindsight. Patience isn't the same thing as experience, but they usually come in a matched pair. Not available by mail order.

It always starts the same way: A simple love of horses. It's the most magical thing and it will half-kill both of you. There's a reaction that happens when that love is mixed with a moment of equine confusion: Bewilderment, which can be easily mistaken for disobedience. Time speeds up, breathing goes shallow and lofty training goals degenerate into a wrestling match.

Impatience is when your brain has a runaway to the land of fear, resistance, and frustration and drags your horse along. Horses reflect these feelings so quickly that we think it was them in the first place. Now who's confused?

I am all for a gallop where our hearts soar with freedom and confidence. I notice a lot of us fall short of that *Black Beauty* fantasy. Can we all agree on one fundamental fact? Horses cannot learn if they are afraid or confused. The best work is volunteered.

If that last statement makes you tilt your head to the side and perk up your ears like a corgi who hears kibble hit the kitchen floor, then you might be ready to take your riding to the next level. First you will need even more patience.

Patience is the ability to control time and influence outcome. Doesn't that almost sound like world domination? Patience is not just simply the ability to stay present in the moment, it's how we behave in that moment. It's the ability to breathe really deeply into a teeny split-second and expand it large enough, and make it slothful enough, to give you all the time you need to stay peacefully connected with your horse. Patience isn't a verb, it's a near Zen-like state of being where time slows and partnership grows. It is the one quality that raises any equine endeavor to an art form.

On the low side, patience doesn't tolerate being hurried, shoved around, or jerked onto the bit. Go figure.

Recipe for Patience

(You want to make this from scratch, the store-bought kind doesn't hold up.)

Ingredients: Start with one fresh, crisp horse and add one rider with heart and commitment.

Mix together with all the time in the world. It's elastic, let it be any size and shape when you start. Stir in positive training techniques and moisten with compassion for the horse and kindness for yourself. Strengthen with a shot of passion. Season generously with humility. Add a pinch of humor to make that last ingredient more palatable.

Mix with intestinal fortitude; you get that from your grandmother. Blend smoothly with consistency and fairness. Grease the way with understanding. Sweeten to taste with organic gratitude. Turn out and cover with acceptance. Let it rise to double and bake in the saddle to a golden color.

Serve with soft hands to the world. This is what riding horses with compassion looks like: a partnership where both sides feast on the best in each other. Then cut into small pieces of memory that last longer than the years we have with that horse. Carry them in your heart forever so that other horses can recognize it in you.

Does this all sound just too fussy for you? It isn't too late to switch over to riding something with an ignition.

Patience, also known as living in horse time. May you dwell there forever.

Top 10 Reasons to Love Riding in the Wind List

The advantages of *not* having an indoor arena on the flat, windy, treeless plains of Colorado:

10. Less time is spent working the arena—all hoof prints are erased hourly, along with the top inch of sand.

9. Wind speeds up spring grooming, stripping hair out like a brand new shedding blade.

8. Riding with feel is increased as your goggles get covered with dust or you simply ride with your eyes closed in one direction .

7. Un-cued, near Rollkur-like vertical head position while going into a headwind, horse and rider alike.

6. Lateral wind helps aid half pass training—as well as going *very deep* into the downwind corners.

5. Maintaining the rhythm of gaits on a circle in high winds makes riding *ANY OTHER TIME* effortless.

4. Halt into a head wind in one stride, followed by a back-up like a reining horse.

3. No need for rider to pay for expensive microderm abrasion skin treatments.

2. Mares will extend the trot with a *wind-up-your-skirt* sort of forward.

1. Gain a more balanced seat dodging the new neighbor's flying lawn chairs, trash cans and wading pools. (Any fear of plastic bags was resolved long ago.)

Is belligerent optimism an oxymoron?

Volunteering 101: Come Get Me

This week spring hit the Colorado prairie. You can tell because the temperature and the wind speed are the same. Tumble weeds broke into my barn and sure, Edgar Rice Burro eats them like Cheetos, but there's only so much even he can do. Tumbleweeds are so deep in the gelding pen that the boys are sleeping on them like prickly feather beds.

I've written about the benefits of riding in the wind but it hasn't caught on yet. Consequently, lessons were canceled and I had some extra time to spend in my Pen for Wayward Ponies. Meet Pippi, here from Ruby Ranch Horse Rescue. She's new this week. See those flattened hairs over her nose. Yes, she came in a halter with a tab dangling. You know what that means...

I love my work and I get to train some fancy and challenging things, but hands down, my absolute favorite thing to train is this: I walk into the pen holding a halter and lead and say, "Come get me." At first Pippi gave me a lovely view of her hind end complete with a madly flashing tail. You know what that means, too. A week later and I'm getting a more attractive view. She has very sweet eyes when she isn't afraid.

What do you believe? Is there any reason a horse shouldn't have as good a recall as a dog? Or depending on breed, even better? Recall with horses and dogs start at the same place; coming to their human should be fun and happy.

This seems obvious enough, but most of us sleepwalk through this part or are in such a hurry to get in the saddle that we forget our manners. Take a moment and listen. If your horse avoids you, passively or actively, he's being honest. It's the clearest way he has to let you know he isn't happy. Do you think it's just a random habit that doesn't mean anything? That's okay, but when it's reflected later in the quality of his work, connect the dots. If we want them responsive to a smaller cue, then we have to do the same.

On the threshold of the pen is where the relationship begins each day. We set the tone for everything that follows and it could be the most telling and important moment of your work session. Does your horse volunteer? Do you give him a chance?

At the very least, ask for his eye, ask his permission before the halter. Wait and breathe. Give him a chance to take a step toward you. Check your body language, cock a hip and give him a minute to volunteer. If he does, lots of reward before the halter. Remember that catching a horse doesn't actually have much to do with a halter at all. I like to rest the lead rope over his neck and thank him for catching *me*.

Most of all, don't act like a coyote; don't think you can stalk him with the halter hidden. You aren't fooling anyone, least of all your horse. It's fundamentally dishonest and you can do better. Pay attention to your feet. The more you move them, the more he will run. Go slow, one step at a time. He knows what's going on, give him some respect. If you need to, move him into a smaller pen to start. Take the drama and chase out of the equation and the conversation improves right away.

If he's resistant, begin the practice of *not* catching him. Carry the halter out with you and take as much time as you need until he volunteers a little bit. Reward him for that lavishly and turn and leave. Mess with his mind in a good way. And don't be surprised if he starts to follow you.

Does he come every time when you shake that can of grain? Good start. I use treats as rewards, but involve yourself deeper than that. Make sure the treat works as a training aid to better behavior and not a license for poor ground manners while you wrestle the halter on. If he grabs the treat and runs, it isn't working. Sometimes replace the treat with long moments of scratching his favorite spot. In other words, *you* be the treat. I have three diminutive equines here now, and all of them are learning to catch me. Breezy, the pony, has the longest distance to come. He got baited with treats and then pounced on, so treats actually scare him. Treats are his cue that something bad is about to happen. The only thing scarier than treats are people who act like coyotes while giving treats. Breezy wants to remind you that honesty is always the best policy.

If the devil is in the details, then an angel must be there, too. Change, either good or bad, starts small. Good horsemanship requires even a reluctant and somewhat lazy human to see a can-of-worms horse behavior that would be easier to ignore, as an opportunity for creative communication and mutual partnership.

Dressage on a Rescue:
Doing More with Less

I have a confession. I shop-lifted when I was in high school. No, I don't seem like the type. It was the only time I ever stole anything and what they say is right: Willfully breaking the law impacts your character.

I was in a pet store and there was a tiny kitten much too young to be weaned. Black and white, skin and bones, crusty eyes and congested; I couldn't stand it. I took her out of the cage and headed for the front door.

I didn't consider hiding her; instead I cuddled her up close to my face. Her tiny lungs were wheezing. A clerk tried to stop me, "You have to pay for that!" He called the kitten *that*. In a teen voice filled with righteous indignation, I hissed, "This kitten is dying," and didn't break stride until I hit the car. Yes, I was silly enough to think I would hear sirens and get arrested in the parking lot. I brought her home and marched past my mother—it wasn't hard to gauge her level of enthusiasm—and into my room. I made a bed in a shoe box with a hot water bottle and a towel, and fed her some warm milk with an eye dropper. She gulped it down and let loose with a rattling, phlegm-laden purr. And I was right, she died that night. I flatter myself that I made a tiny difference, but not the life of that doomed kitten. The difference was in me.

In some ways, dressage is a very elite sport. It is a wonderful thing to see an FEI horse competing in his prime—the best training on an impeccably bred Warmblood, guided by a talented rider, and brought along with all the advantages.

But I love the practicality of dressage, as well as the art. For me, the real question is how much dressage training can help off-the-track Thoroughbreds, smart Arabians, or whatever horse you ride now. The magic of dressage is the balance, relaxation, and strength it provides for any horse, at any age, and in any discipline. I love an animated piaffe and positively swoon for a great canter half-pass. But in my heart, the true beauty of dressage is the *practical usefulness* it gives a horse with less advantage. It's just more interesting.

"I have...always been criticized for not buying good and sound animals for myself, as other masters do. But to educate such an animal teaches the rider nothing. It is too easy. The master does not prove his own ability nor the practical usefulness of his art by training horses already made nearly perfect by nature. The test of his science and his utility lies in his ability to correct the natural defects of an ordinary animal and make it useful." —Henri L. De Bussigny, 1922.

So my dressage world is very inclusive: I have clients who are endurance riders and eventers. Some are gaited horses and I have had the extreme advantage of working with mules and donkeys. I work with clients who have challenging horses who flunked out or were dismissed by other trainers. Western tack has been used in my lessons long before there was a name for it, and best of all, lots of my clients have rescue horses: Off the track Thoroughbreds, PMU babies, and horses that fell between the cracks. Whether they came from a rescue organization, or were one step away—but for the luck of being saved. The common thread in this eclectic herd is that the riders want to build a better horse, rather than buy one.

Sadly, I don't see as many dressage riders pick rescue horses as I would like. And bluntly put, if you want the highest scores in this sport, buy a Warmblood. But if you don't have plans for the Olympics… If the truth is that you'll never be a world-class rider on a world-class horse, then why not do life-changing work? Ride a rescue.

Because in the end, all the money in the world can't buy the ride. Or the relationship. These are things that must be earned and every step is not beautiful, but in the end it is the stuff of horse legend. Remember *Seabiscuit*: "You don't throw a whole life away just 'cuz he's banged up a little."

Which finally brings me to my point: A client, who rides a rescue horse and wants to do Western dressage, sent me a link to the International Rescue Horse Registry, LLC. You can find them on Facebook and on the USDF website. It means that your rescue horse can qualify for end-of-the-year awards. The organization has been around for over a year, but I hadn't heard and maybe you haven't either. It's time to take some pride in doing the right thing, for the horse and eventually the sport in general.

Contact: Holding Hands with Horses

What is the world's speed record for learning to ride on happy contact? Eighteen years? Maybe twenty-three? It's a joke about contact but see what I mean? It isn't funny. Nothing about contact is funny; it's really difficult. It's the sort of frustration that makes a rider want to take up insanely precise and complicated needle-point just for a breath of fresh air. Or any of the other suggestions your horse gives you because he can't stand how *hard* you are trying to learn kindness with your hands.

Good contact flows so seamlessly that the horse *feels as if* he's on a long rein. What can possibly go wrong?

Trainers try to explain contact with various words like vibrate and jiggle. I lose rhythm just saying them, much less trying to figure out what they mean on a rein. But we all know the tense ugliness of hard contact.

Some trainers just go for the quick and dirty answer: Pull and kick even harder. It's a choice we make; either see the horse get his face jerked erratically or watch your client get so frustrated that they can't remember their name.

Contact is the biggest challenge that most of my clients struggle with. Every trainer is different, every rider is different, and then each horse is a unique sentient being. In the end, the horse's opinion of your contact is the only one that counts.

The problem with focusing on hand contact is that the most important area of contact is always our seat. We ride with our whole body and there's a bizarre mutually exclusive rule that comes into play while learning something new. Do you know it? Say you're riding rhythmically along but you have to engage your brain on a task with your hands, and then your seat stops as soon as your brain starts. Your horse, however, never forgets your seat, even when you do. And so he obediently slows to a halt and reminds you one more time, we ride with our seats...

It's easy to tell if your contact isn't working. Your hands inhibit your horse, more than him striding from behind pushes him on. As confused as self-defeating as riding the brake while using the gas pedal in a car. When you think of it that way, it's a loss of balance between the hind and the poll. There's no pulling a horse back to the bit, you have to let him go forward to the bit. It's just one more of the counter-intuitive things about riding and the list is long! Does your brain hurt yet?

Once you understand the semi-technical things, like closed fingers and thumbs up and how to adjust reins, then you have to empty your over-thinking mind and just ride it. Nothing kills rhythm like needing to think about the next time to clap along with the beat of the music. It's time to stop counting and start dancing.

It isn't hard to pull up a mental image of a horse gliding forward at liberty with a gently arched neck, an unrestricted poll, and fluid movement. In order to get that beauty under saddle, a rider has to flow with her horse seamlessly. She can not pull against him and disturb the rhythm, she must find a way to release with his movement. Connecting in that rhythm is when riding looks easy. Which is a totally different thing than simple.

Remember, most of all, in dressage we never bump a bit against the horse's mouth or see-saw the bit back and forth. Never become complacent about the force exerted by even a gentle bit—it's still metal on bone. Period. We want the horse to embrace that connection with us, so the bit is never, not-ever-even-once, used for punishment. Other riding disciplines do, but we don't. It is one of the things that sets us apart and we need to take some pride in that. No matter how frustrated it makes us.

There is no shortage of techniques but in the end, it's about feel. Oh, great. More abstractions when all a rider wants is a direct action that works every time.

When your brain is thick, dragged down with words and theories and severe effort, the horse's steps drag. The forced techniques run together so much that your hands rebel from their own wrists and all you can do is pull. His trot feels like dragging a box of rocks and a canter would be impossible to launch as a school bus from a slingshot... then just ride. Move forward, drop the reins, and feel him striding under you. Forward with freedom and elasticity—just like the dressage test reads. Let him carry you, just ride. When you pick up the reins again, breath in art and exhale freedom.

There is an art to holding hands, too. Have you held hands with someone who has more tension in their arm than rhythm, someone who carries your hand just a bit high, or pushes the swing past a natural place or goes from fluid to abrupt in a disturbing stride? It's the tense pull of your mother's hand when you were little and in trouble. The teenage angst-filled hand of your first date. Or it's the hand that moves and flows so fluidly that the two of you move unified in a rhythm that balances tides and moon phases. A rhythm as slow and still as a primeval swamp and as weightless as a glide to the moon.

Contact is like holding hands with someone you are so comfortable with, that there's overlap where they begin and you end. It happens when minds and hearts are swept away in an effortless beat of rhythm. Contact is the place between individuals where respect and love embrace.

Good contact is moving forward through space without gravity or dependence on anything more concrete than the flow of movement that is oneness.

Training Confidence and Trust

There's a way that a mare can pin her ears back so hard that they make almond-shaped divots on her neck hairs. You don't have to know much about horses to pick up on that cue. It's big and dark and she looks like a fanged serpent. By the time this is happening, there's even an argument she will have a hard time hearing you, literally, what with her ear drums smashed into her poll and all.

The other laundry list of signs that your horse is upset include flared nostrils, wide tense eyes with too much white showing and short, shallow breaths. It's almost common sense if you pay attention.

We are all so clear about the signs a horse is coming apart, but do you recognize the signs that your horse is confident, relaxed, or just comprehending things? Are his ears relaxed and moving forward and back? Is his neck long and his poll soft; are his eyes big and fluid? Is his tail clamped down or swinging with his spine when he moves?

Beginning to learn horse language is dangerous if we over-simplify and humanize the horse, meaning dumb him down and miss his message. Is all of this head shoving and mugging on the ground affection or is he insecure? It's flattering to think it's affection, but a confident horse who stands flat and relaxed is the best reflection of the horse/rider relationship. How do we train that kind of confidence?

Is he blowing to tell you his back feels good and he is ready to work? If not, you have more warm up work to do. Is he blinking his eyes, thinking about what he has just learned? If he is, give him a minute—and that means stand still and respect his process of learning. A conversation, by definition, means listening, too.

If the horse gets confused, are you certain that you aren't giving him a mixed signal? Is your body awareness so perfect that you are incapable of contradicting yourself in horse language? Are you listening to yourself as closely as your horse is? Now the conversation is getting more personal.

Are you so sure that he is pulling on the reins because he wants to run off with you, or is he just feeling so much pressure on the bit, metal on bone, that he is tossing his head trying to breathe and stretch his neck? Or are your reins a little loose and is he tossing his head, trying to make contact? What quality of *hand shake* with the reins does your individual horse want? Firm and fluid is the answer, but what does *that* translate to in terms of feel and finesse? Now the conversation is getting really intimate.

In order to progress with your horse, it isn't so much training a specific technical movement as it is training confidence and trust to do the movement correctly. The difference between a frantic explosive canter depart and a smooth soft uphill canter depart reveals more about the quality of the horse/rider relationship than anything else.

This is where the *art* comes in. Can you speak in his language and influence him in a positive way? A good place to start is acknowledging (rewarding) positive communication. If he is moving forward, follow his movement softly, but stop with the leg cue. When he blows, say *good boy*. Reward him for trying, and ask for a tiny bit more. Say thank you and repeat. Score extra points for patience, a key ingredient in confidence building.

Remember: The things we focus on and reward are the things that grow—good or bad. The foundation of dressage is rhythm and maybe the emotional definition of rhythm is confidence and trust in movement. Horses love rhythm: it's included in all good things like breathing, chewing, walking in the sun, and excluded in all bad or scary things like bucking, spooking, or bolting. Rhythm is a rider's very best friend and training aid.

So if you are having a conversation with a horse that includes praise of going forward and praise of being relaxed, you are in a much better negotiating position, whether you are training a new movement in an arena or out on the trail. Not only is a relaxed and forward horse easier to stay on, but they get over emotional disturbances more quickly because they want to return to the safe place their leader has for them. External challenges are less interesting because the horse is so comfortable and safe *in rhythm* with his rider. Soon spooking disturbs that conversation, and isn't worth the effort.

The difference between micro-managing a horse's every move and having a conversation with a horse might seem like semantics, but not to a horse. It's the difference between leadership that says "Do what I say immediately and correctly or suffer the consequences of my anger," or "Let's work together, I will listen to your concerns and we will work this out safely and sanely." It's the difference between soul-killing obedience and a happy, relaxed, and forward ride.

What Does the Horsie Say? Seriously

Our barn rat, Hannah, didn't meet the horses on her first visit to the farm. She was only three days old. We waited till her second visit later that week. It was love at first sight for all of us. By the time she was toddling and learning to talk, she knew all the horse's names. Her parents taught her the animal sound game, "What does a horsie say?" Hannah's answer was a high-pitched, arching trill, ""Nei-ay-ay-agh!" Her voice is so high that it is almost inaudible to anyone but the dogs.

Warning: Do not be fooled by Hannah's tutu. Don't let her pink-themed wardrobe distract you. Don't let the near toxic level of cuteness cancel out the message.

With the parent's game over, Hannah wandered down the stall row and came to Grace's pen. The mare met her at the gate with her nose toddler high and gave her one of those deep growl-y mare nickers. Almost a moan, slow and quiet. And Hannah answered her back. The toddler's voice dropped so low that she almost sounded possessed. Which she clearly was, but not in a bad way. "Uuh-oo-oo-uuh" came from behind Hannah's belly button and barely cleared her lips. But Grace heard it.

Hannah is bi-lingual. She has one answer for humans, and a separate answer for horses. She's that smart.

Disclaimer: I think kids are kind of in the same boat as mini horses. They are fully complete, sentient creatures who know as much as anyone else and deserve respect, but we see them as pint-sized caricatures of the real thing and diminish them.

What if Hannah shares that deep well of intuitive knowledge that horses do, and just lacks the superficial communication skills that we adults use? The horses seem to think she is communicating fine.

Most of us have had that experience of seeing horses take care of little kids—the same horses that are a total handful for adults who theoretically know how to ride. At the same time, we remember riding as kids, free and effortless. We knew less and got more from our horses. When did riding get so complicated? What have we forgotten?

Hannah is right, we do need to use a separate language for horses. They don't speak English just because they can take a canter cue from the word *Canter!* Responding to a verbal cue is good; maybe it was the actual word they understood, or your body language before the word? We can chatter away at them; we can coo and cluck with our horses and feel just great. Don't mistake that with a real relationship based in a shared language beyond words, spoken with our bodies and our intentions. A trainer can't literally teach relationship, they can only try to inspire a rider to feel it, and then acknowledge it when a horse and rider have the experience. Trainers are translators and facilitators. The real relationship has be first-hand communication.

If humans are the more evolved species (and the jury is out on that, but going with that assumption) then it is up to us to move beyond our more limited senses and evolve our language to meet the horse. More importantly, if we want to progress farther with our horses, we have to communicate even more eloquently. Just getting louder doesn't work.

How many times do we climb on a horse and then talk about him behind his back? We sit in the saddle and ignore him, while we have an intense mental conversation with ourselves about our horses. We check mental lists of technique and we put dark thought into anxiety or worry. Our critical thoughts run like a rat on a wheel, while we pander to our worst opinions of ourselves.

How is the ride going so far? Is this any different than texting and driving?

Let's focus on *us* first. Take a body check. Are you sound? Is your body soft and open, or does tension in your shoulders cut off you off at the neck? Are your hips tight and restrictive on the ground? Don't expect a horse to do his best work if you are lame or stiff.

Slow down, take some time, and breathe. Inflate your ribs, let them be elastic. Exhale out the day's drama. Inhale and know that you have all the time you need. Exhale out any erratic human emotions. Inhale and know you are fine as you are. Exhale and feel balance in your body. Here and now, reset yourself to less judgment and more acceptance. Less thinking and more feeling. Less correction, more direction. Be. Here. Now.

By the time you get to the mounting block, know that you are crossing a border into another country. You can play the ugly American, talking loud and looking for a McDonalds for lunch, or you can open your mind and learn the local customs. The best trips are the ones where both sides respect and learn. And the sum of these parts make a better world.

It's the one thing that all my clients say they want most of all: A better relationship with their horse. Take a cue from Hannah. If you want to have a more elite connection with your horse, develop your nicker.

Meanwhile, Hannah and Grace are still at the gate. It isn't about treats, and it isn't that the mare can't leave if she wants. They are being together. They are acknowledging each other by sharing breath, sharing time, and sharing their heart's language. Existing in the present moment without expectations or demands is an art form. Respect the masters.

Getting Happy About What You Don't Know

Most of us started as back yard riders. No shame, we were kids, we climbed up and rode. When we fell off, we climbed up and rode some more. I must have known there was tack, I watched Westerns on TV after all, but we didn't own any. We thought you kicked a horse to make him trot and if you wanted to canter, you kicked even harder, and maybe flung yourself forward while pulling up on his face. No, not pretty, but we all had to start somewhere and our horses taught us to ride better. Some of us took the cue with more grace than others, and when we knew better, we did better. Some of us were more defensive and adversarial; we enjoyed the drama and adrenaline of a fight. Do you know someone like that? The other word for it is *bully*.

Learning is a vulnerable position. It involves listening with an open mind and a willingness to consider the big picture. Learning is a desire to look past the surface of how things work to the inter-relationship of the parts, to reason, and creatively participate. Learning while sitting on top of a thousand pound horse, who has thoughts and emotions of his own, complicates things.

It's easy to have sensory overwhelm in the saddle and tell our brains to shut down the information intake. In riding, an over-controlling or closed mind is the enemy of sensitivity. It takes us out of the conversation with the horse in the moment and into a conversation with our own brains about the horse. It's a huge difference; it's going from talking *to* them to talking *about* them. We want to balance on the tight wire between sensing physically and thinking emotionally. It's the difference between responding and reacting; one is inclusive and one is defensive. Did I mention that this is only a tight wire wide?

Here is where I remind you riding is an art. It's supposed to be challenging.

At the same time, some of us think that leadership is about domination. I understand the attraction to this sort of training. It's black and white. The rider has control, by using dominance, to correct what's already in the past.

Example: The horse is tossing his head, so she pulls on his face. He pulls more, so she bumps with the bit. He flinches, his poll gets tense, and he pushes for some relief, she corrects his face with aggressive hands. Each toss gets more tense, each correction more punishing. She's stopped listening to her horse, now he's getting a lesson in fight and resistance. And we humans have an innate urge to dominate, maybe even more so when we're intimidated. It feels like a natural response. How's this working?

In dressage requirements and tests, there is a movement to change the word submission to cooperation. Great idea!

"You don't make him learn, you set it up to allow him to learn. You have to give him that with dignity. Once you start giving, you won't believe how much you get back." Ray Hunt, dressage master in different tack.

In the same example, if the rider comes from a standpoint of learning, being open with her senses, the conversation can take place in the present. Rather than correcting the last mistake, the horse/rider can negotiate. If the horse tugs, you might be reminded that your hand has become set; you can take the cue to follow his movement better, encouraging the horse to move forward more. It stops being black or white, right or wrong, good or bad. Instead the lines become more flexible, senses more aware and both minds are openly communicating. This is the exact spot in which brilliance is possible. Art can happen. In this place, vulnerability is our greatest strength; a positive willingness to let the horse to do what we ask.

Again, most of us started in our backyards. We didn't know how much we didn't know. We just wanted to ride. If we kept at it, we looked for markers of our skill. Here's my rule of thumb: A rider who thinks they are right is a rank beginner. A master in the saddle is one who is vulnerable to learning.

It was noted that Nuno Oliveira, the Portuguese Master, rode very hunched over during the last years of his life and yet he became a better rider; his horses were also more relaxed and brilliant. He remarked that it was a pity that his back was giving up "because it is now that I am beginning to learn how to ride a horse."

Calming Signals:
Are You Listening?

If you are standing next to your horse and he looks away, do you think he's distracted or even disrespectful? When your horse yawns, is he sleepy or bored? If he moves slowly, is he lazy? These are important cues from your horse; are you hearing him correctly?

When it comes to communicating with horses, some humans are a bit like a self-obsessed rock star who throws a temper tantrum and trashes the room, but then assumes everyone wants his autograph. By equine standards, we ignore those around us and begin by screaming bloody-murder and escalate from there. Part of respecting a horse is remembering that their senses are much keener than ours. We can whisper.

"It is just like man's vanity and impertinence to call an animal dumb because it is dumb to his dull perceptions." —Mark Twain.

Horses give us *calming signals*, just like dogs. Norwegian dog trainer and behaviorist Turid Rugaas wrote about it in 2005. She coined the phrase *calming signals* to describe the social skills, or body language, that dogs use to avoid conflict, invite play, and communicate a wide range of information to other dogs.

Calming signals in horses are somewhat similar and include looking away, having lateral ears, yawning, stretching down, licking lips or eating to calm themselves. Can you recognize them? Calming cues communicate stress, and at the same time, release stress. They're modeling behavior for us; they want us to drop our stress level, or aggressiveness, as well.

When a horse looks away, either with his eyes or whole head and neck, it is a calming cue. He uses a signal like this when he feels pressured and wants the rider to know he senses the person's agitation or aggression, but that person can calm down because he is no threat to the human. In the horse's mind, he is communicating clearly and with respect.

Do you pull his head back and force his position? It's human nature to turn up our volume if we think we aren't being heard and maybe the hardest thing about listening to calming signals is that they kind of poke our dominant parts. So when the horse signals us to be less aggressive, but we mistakenly hear it as boredom or distraction or even disobedience, and then follow that up with a larger cue, we're starting a fight. We're letting the horse know we choose aggression over peace. Is that what you meant to say? Or is the appropriate positive response from a good leader to de-escalate the situation?

"It is just like man's vanity and impertinence to call an animal dumb because it is dumb to his dull perceptions." —Mark Twain. (It deserves repeating.)

If riders want to understand the language of horses, we need stop seeing our horses in our own worst image (lazy or distracted) and begin a conversation where we listen more openly, more honestly. It's much too simplistic to lump every-thing a horse does into either dominant or submissive behavior. Herd life has much more nuance than that. As social animals, they work to get along, encouraging others to cooperate. Even dominant boss mares give calming cues.

We can build trust with the horse if we learn to respect calming signals, and even reward them. In my training, the best calming signal I have is my breath. I can slow it down, emphasize the exhale, and just be still at the end. Using breath is a huge aid that horses pay attention to, so much more than humans realize.

Each time I start work with a horse, I ask for his eye, using my eye. I want him to volunteer. If my horse looks away, I take a deep breath, acknowledge the moment, and go slow. Usually on my second or third breath, he'll look back and tell me he's ready. It's a short wait, compared to putting fear or resistance in that eye.

Reading horse body language takes some quiet time to learn, and they aren't all exactly alike. Some horses are so shut down, so overwhelmed by us pounding on them in the past, that they have no calming cues at all, but you can remind him. Calming is a good thing, no matter who cues it.

If you are thinking of tuning up your communication skills with your horse, I really recommend ground work. It's my favorite thing about the Horse Agility we do here at Infinity Farm. Obstacles are great conversation starters with a horse, and if the human can get past needing to dominate the obstacle, communication can be eloquent, with understanding and a healthy give-and-take reasoning. And it all translates to the saddle later.

Now that I think about it, when I meet someone who is loud or aggressive, I tend to look away, too. Sometimes I turn my shoulders sideways and don't make eye contact. I notice I don't like aggressive people crowding me and talking loud either. This is about the time I become aware that I do groundwork with humans as often as I do horses. Maybe the real reason we shouldn't humanize horses is because they had it right in the first place.

It's a Riding Lesson. What Could Possibly Go Wrong?

It starts innocently enough, just like every other thing that happens around horses. A rider might have a problem with their horse, or maybe a goal. It sounds innocent enough.

Then there's the horse, maybe he's confused or maybe he's bored. No blame, no fault. He's being honest and if you don't like what he is saying, lessons are a good idea.

The rider might have grown up with horses and worked with lots of trainers or she might be just starting with horses, lessons, and this whole world.

Start here: She loves her horse. No, *really*, as if I need convincing, she tells me how great her horse is. I never disagree, it's pretty easy for me to find something to like about an equine, but more than that, no one calls a trainer for help because they hate their horse. Then she probably tells me one more really wonderful thing about how they got together or some big success in the past. She's getting closer to telling me more about the problem, which might feel almost be like a betrayal. "He's a great horse, but he…" It can be a precarious place for a rider, being critical of the horse who inspires their passion. At the same time that they want me to like him, they want me to see what's wrong with him too.

Visualize a field of land mines for all concerned. In this infinite world of horses, there is one thing every single one of us has in common: massive, huge, and over-sized feelings about our horses. What could possibly go wrong?

Insert a trainer: I meet the rider and listen. I meet the horse and listen. They usually tell different versions of the same story. I try to establish a common language. This part is tricky, even if we all speak English, no one seems to define the words the same way. If you don't believe me, ask two people to define contact. Or forward. Or leadership. See?

Here is where I go into my Building Inspector mode: I check the foundation for loose bricks and cracks. Is the horse sound, does the tack fit? How is the emotional foundation of the horse? Are there any symptoms of a sour stomach or ulcers? This is such a common challenge in riding horses and since the first signs are usually behavioral, a trainer might see them before a vet sometimes. This first step never varies: If the horse is not sound, his behavior is the only way he has to communicate that to you. It would be a huge mistake to *train* his symptoms away rather than listen and help.

If I am certain that the horse is sound and the tack is not abusive, I try to find a light-hearted and cheerful way to let the rider know the good news: it's something they are doing. Sometimes the rider translates that to *my fault*. Harsh words, and a sense of humor is pretty important right about now. But what did you expect? Was I supposed to compliment you and your horse, tell you the problem was imaginary, and ask for my check?

It's actually good news! If it's something you are doing, it can change. Communication can improve, balance can become more solid, and confidence can grow. Some of us have herds of retired or lame horses, and we'd be thrilled to think we could change that by just riding better.

Here is the truth: Riding well is hard. Horses are not dirt bikes—if you want to improve your partnership with your horse, it is something you will work on forever. Dressage riders are eternal students of the horse, we never stop learning. There is no stigma about lessons, it is just a matter of course if you are serious about horses. So no guilt, no apologies.

You are training your horse each time you ride.

It's an old adage and we have all heard it so much it sounds trite. Well, it's just flat out true.

I hear riders sometimes talk about their lessons as punishment, that their trainers yell and they are constantly corrected. Some of us have trainer horror stories; I certainly do. No trainer can be right for every client and first lessons are always a bit stressful, but shop around and find someone who makes sense to your ears. Let your horse have a vote, too. There are some trainers out there who really don't like horses much. I know; it shocks me, too.

This is the biggest thing I know: Horses thrive on rhythm. All bad things, like spooking, bucking, or bolting are a loss of that natural calming movement. It's no coincidence that the foundation of dressage training pyramid is rhythm, and a horse can't have relaxed and forward gaits with a tense or upset rider, so my first priority is to put the rider at ease. And then get ready to say *good boy*—this is supposed to be fun!

Am I shamelessly promoting riding lessons to line my pockets with your hard-earned cash? No. Every week I'm reminded that there is a very fine line between a well-loved family horse and a horse abandoned to rescue or his lonely pasture. The difference is only a few lessons.

Horse Agility and Calming Signals

It's that time again. I fill a cart at the dollar store and a glimpse in the rear view mirror while driving away looks like a clown exploded in the extended cab of my truck. Then the wading pool comes out of the rafters and I dust off the bubble makers. Cones, barrels, and hula-hoops make their way to the pasture, and I hang my favorite sign: Snakes in the Llama Room.

Horse Agility is back! Or I could call it a Calming Signal Event and really elevate the conversation. Horses would come running.

Horse agility is a game of partnership without coercion. Most of us have done obstacles in-hand with our horses, but Horse Agility is different. The eventual goal is to work off lead, just like dogs do. So we begin using a long, loose lead rope and just like dog agility, we do the asking and the animal does the obstacle. Instead of leading the horse over the obstacle, we send the horse while we stand at a small distance.

Begin with leading exercises. And *since we all know there is no pulling on his face,* that means we cue with breath and body language. Begin by asking for his eye with your eye. If he looks toward you, reward him with a scratch and a kind word. If he looks away, it's a calming signal. His way of saying he is no threat, which means he thinks you're acting aggressively. Or at the least, loud.

For crying out loud, you say, I am just holding the rope! If you think you are not pushing, and he acts *as if* you are, who wins? You want to get this right; if the first step of working initiates a fight, you will never get his best work. At this moment you are setting a tone for the day. Go slow and give him a chance to volunteer. He might be slightly braced, waiting for you to pull on the rope. Just don't do it. Take a breath or two, and he will look back. Then reward him while you feel the entire universe shift toward partnership. It's a quiet internal feeling that might take a minute to recognize, on both sides.

Walk on, out of his space, and cue with your inhale and your feet. Halt with an exhale and stop your feet. Reward lavishly; let him know you like his listening. The lead rope may only be used as a last resort, then just a slack jiggle or a quick ask and release. You might have a feeling of being impaired or disabled without the rope, but that's *your* cue that you over-cue by habit.

If your horse looks a bit confused at this point, it's because he is a bit surprised by your peaceful cues and he might need a moment to thank the horse gods. This is the perfect time to reward him, go slow and stick with him. Reward any slight movement in the right direction. Instead of punishing him for looking away or going slow or seeming distracted, hear him. Acknowledge his calming cues and find a smaller, quieter way to ask. Then feel the universe shift one more time. It feels small at the beginning, almost like you're imagining it.

Start with an easy obstacle and listen to your horse. Walk up to a simple tarp or a hula hoop on the ground. Now, resist the temptation to manipulate him with the lead; instead stand out of his space and send him over it by asking his hind leg to step forward. Almost as if you were lunging him, use the end of your rope and send him forward toward the obstacle while you stand still. Remember the foundation of dressage is rhythmic movement; the art in agility is that same relaxed mind and body.

He calmly crosses and you reward his quiet success. Next time, halt him half-way over without pulling the rope. Your horse especially likes the no pulling clause here. Exhale him to a stop, and let your body language rest. That release is the reward.

Walk away and take a break. Next go, how about backing him over, again with a long rope with quiet cues. Can you ask his left hind hoof to stand on the tarp, step by step, by sending and breathing?

Here's the secret: Approach every obstacle the exact same way, whether it's a wading pool with invisible ankle-biting trout or a seemingly two-inch wide teeter. Never let the obstacle be bigger than the conversation with your horse. Then ride that way too. I know, I know: The simple things are never easy.

Obstacles are not pass/fail tests. In fact, the obstacle isn't the point at all. Sometimes people drag horses through the course like it's a race and the horses have a glazed look, resisting the rush. Are you pulling on his face? One reason it matters is that if you do it on the ground, you probably do it in the saddle too. Maybe you have dominated all obstacles in record time and you've finished first. I will be just as unimpressed as your horse. If you want speed and confidence, understanding has to come first and going slow is the fastest way to get it.

The goal in agility is sweet partnership, in a soft relaxed and forward way, with the horse doing the work and the handler quietly asking. Sounds like dressage to me: Ground dressage.

Any horse, any size, any age can do it, but are you fit enough for Horse Agility? I mean emotionally fit, of course. The secret to agility, or anything else with a horse, is maintaining a calm energy. Can you stay present in the moment with your horse without distraction or frustration? Can you lead with positive confidence? The first obstacle is always our own attitude.

Training is Like a
Box of Chocolates…

Say hello to Mr. Mustache. That's what I call him. He was relinquished to Ruby Ranch Horse Rescue and my barn was his first stop. To say he didn't get out much is an understatement. He's six and this is his first time away from his mom. With very minimal handling in the past, he isn't all that attached to people but at the same time, not really wild. He has a lot to teach me.

When he first came he seemed extremely distracted. Even after a couple of days to relax, his eye was still small and he didn't care to connect. It was kind of like the thing the popular girls used to do in my high school: Look right through you while scanning the room for someone interesting. Do you know that invisible feeling? Only in this case, he banged his jawbone on my skull in the process. Should I punish him? It's very rude.

One of the best lessons I know about training horses I learned from a puppy back when I was nineteen. She was not house-broken when she came to me and I was patient. I watched and took her into the yard at the right times, and rewarded her for a job well done. She learned fast and didn't make mistakes. I was some dog trainer, housebroken in just a couple of days.

In the evening we took long walks and she always wanted to get into the yard as soon as we got back home. I didn't think much of it. After all, it was nice to not have to pick up after her on the stroll. When she was almost two, we headed out for a road trip in my old VW bug. I stopped after a couple of hours; she didn't need to relieve herself, so off we went. The same thing through the day and by evening she still hadn't relieved herself and I was really concerned. I could see she was stressed. Did I need to get her to a vet?

When she finally relieved herself, she acted so guilty, so nervous that I still worried about her health. Eventually it dawned on me that while I thought that I taught her to not urinate in the house, what she actually learned was to use my back yard, and without that specific back yard, she was undone. She wasn't wrong, surely not disobedient, but we had a difference of perception that mattered all of a sudden. She spent the rest of the trip learning to pee in other people's yards and I learned that training is like a box of chocolates; you never know what you're gonna get. (with apologies to Momma Gump.)

It might be more important to listen to the conversation in training, rather than just focus on the cue and result. Acknowledge the individual and keep an eye on the big picture.

Back to Mr. Mustache. Is his problem a lack of respect for my space? Or is he like most horses, just giving me an honest answer? Maybe what he has learned from people so far is that they are pushy and it gives him anxiety to be around us. Yes, he was in my space but as I watched him, he was a bit shut down to humans all the way around. He was resistant to leading, he didn't want to be touched, and his tail was totally off limits. Maybe his problem was the opposite, he had been pushed away too often.

I always think I have to *buy* the right to correct a horse. To just march into a pen and start being aggressive shuts horses down, just like getting flipped off by an angry driver in rush hour traffic doesn't inspire better driving. First I have to establish a relationship. There has to be some shared focus or why should he care about our conversation in the first place? Most weanlings are born with a curiosity about humans that Mr. Mustache seems to have lost. I won't punish him for that.

"The basic techniques, or what they call basics, are more diffi-cult than what comes later, that is the Trap of Dressage. Correct basics are more difficult than piaffe and passage." —Conrad Schumacher.

I love this quote because what we do right now is always more important that what we might do in the future.

I think Mr. Schumacher was probably referring to forward motion under saddle, but how I translated it to Mr. Mustache was grooming. We started very slow. The curry was too much at first but by the time I finally brushed his tail, we might as well have both been quoting Shakespeare for the elegance of language we had gained. Now his eye is big and soft all the time. He meets me at the gate and by the time I finally put a surcingle on him in the round pen, he could breathe, relax his poll, and stand confidently *outside* of my space.

There are as many training methods as there are riders and as many individual answers as there are horses. If a horse doesn't answer your question correctly, maybe you should try asking a different question. To yourself and your horse.

An Argument Against the Whip

There is a time-worn adage about whips. Just like bits or spurs, whips are only as cruel or kind as the rider using them. Maybe. My mentor rarely rode with a whip, but if she did, she carried two. The most challenging horses loved her. Her corrections were impossibly quick and always fair. She was twice as quick to reward. The conversation with her hands, on the bridle and whip, were eloquent and resistance-free. Riding is an art.

My bad attitude about whips this week is a hold-over from the Belmont. Watching the favorite get wailed on—long and hard on the home stretch—wore me down. Maybe I'm getting old. It's certainly true that I don't understand racing. I've seen jockeys go to the whip with grace and rhythm, perhaps it can be a positive aid. What I saw looked different. To my eye it looked brutal. The crowd cheered, the favorite didn't win, and I gave up watching racing for the hundredth time.

In dressage, whips are allowed at lower levels and the assumption is that all of our aids improve as we go up the levels. We ride on the bit, meaning with our hands in contact with the horse's mouth, metal on bone. If there is anything that takes more sensitivity and focus on the part of the rider, please tell me.

I'm waiting… No, I didn't think so.

Learning good contact is hard and our horses are patient with us in that process. We should return the favor.

The inside hand is the worst culprit; it drags on a horse's

mouth exactly like a parking brake. We all know that good riders use their outside rein, but in the beginning it requires a suspension of disbelief to even give it a try. We humans over-value our opposable thumbs. We think control of a thousand pound-horse is done with our tiny little hand.

Here is how it starts. The horse walks forward and if he feels resistance on the bit, he answers with resistance. He begins to lose forward and his rhythm is compromised. So the rider starts kicking. Now the horse is getting a double message, forward from the rider's leg and halt from her hands. The more we nag with our legs and hold the bit, the more dead to the aids he becomes. So we pick up a whip. Using our previous technique, we train nagging dullness to the whip in no time. In the very worst case scenario, the inside rein gets pulled back to make sharper contact with the whip. Is there a more confusing double message than that? Is it time to bring out the spurs now?

The *emotional arc* of this same scenario starts with nagging a repetitive cue. No releases, no rewards, just pressure and soon nagging turns to frustration in both partners. More aggressive cues fuel a grudge and the frustration grows an edge of resent-ment. The next stop is anger. Is it possible that your horse is as resistant to your attitude as he is your aids?

Asking the same thing louder doesn't make it any more clear. If we inadvertently cue the resistance and the horse loses rhythm in the process, there is some rider fault. And if your hands aren't great in the first place, carrying a whip won't improve them.

What I dislike about using a whip the most in this situation is that it dumbs down the conversation instead of enlightening it. The horse gets rushed. If you aren't getting the answer you want, rather than getting adversarial, why not ask a different question? Set him up to succeed and demonstrate some coop-eration. Encourage your horse by letting the reward be bigger than the ask.

My experience being on the ground teaching is that when I ask the rider to drop the whip, most horses go forward better almost immediately. Either the rider braces less or the horse flinches less, but the result is an improvement.

Instead of an escalation to using more force, how about a smaller cue? I know, it's counter-intuitive, but so much of riding is just that. If resistance trains resistance, then try a softening of the rein as the ask. Think of a small release as the cue. If you are riding on contact, an inch of rein is plenty. Demonstrate softness and not restriction. Your horse will thank you.

Tune up the leg aid and then discipline yourself to keep your leg quiet in between cues. Know that feeling the need to cue every stride is different from following your horse with your seat. It's a flank-deadening nag. Sorry to be blunt.

Let the whip be the last resort. If you are thinking you need a whip, here is the test. Do less; use a neck ring. It can be an old rein or a simple rope tied in a loop. Leave your reins long and use the ring to steer your horse. My rule of thumb says the more frustrated the rider is with the ring, the more she over-controls with her hands. And just to be clear, if the horse improves on a long rein and gets worse when you pick up, it's probably a contact issue. The use of a whip doesn't help your hands. Again, sorry, but I work for your horse.

Is your horse fully warmed up? If a sound horse doesn't want to move forward, he often improves with a more thoughtful mental and physical warm-up; it's the most important part of the ride. This is my annual reminder that dressage and massage rhyme for a reason.

Whips and spurs are not inherently evil but aids really do work at each rider's level of skill. Make sure the ones you use truly elevate the conversation and positively affirm your destination.

Wrestling with Helmet Safety

I almost got in a bar fight a few months back. It was bad: I got frustrated and when that happens, I resort to sarcasm. It was not professional of me, and I would feel better about this whole episode if I was sorry. The problem is that I'm not sorry.

Riders4Helmets International Helmet Awareness Day is coming right up and equestrian retailers around the globe will be offering special one-day only discounts on helmets. I don't get a free helmet for saying so; I just want to remind everyone it's a good time to shop.

Is it getting old? Every year at this time I write about helmet awareness. Some times I write in the horse's voice and some years I try to appeal to common sense. I am most haunted by the blog about my biggest personal fear; meeting a young woman in a nursing home, living a life of disability and mental confusion. She was lost from horses but with just enough memory to miss them. The memory of meeting her still stays in my mind years later.

This has been a rough week in the equestrian world. We lost a couple of elite riders. Whenever we lose people, we want to draw an arbitrary line between them and us, a line that keeps us safe from their fate. "I don't ride horses like that, I don't jump that high." Or it couldn't happen to you because you are safe in another discipline. "I am only a trail rider, I don't even canter."

That's crazy talk, of course. No horse is bomb-proof. Horses are flight animals and in the worst case scenario, instinct can win over training. Where serious injuries on horses are concerned, the disabling or fatal ones are most all head injuries. No surprise, and most active sports require helmets these days. This year it seems there have been more than the usual number of injuries, especially out on the trail. It's hard to come out ahead in a tangle with a thousand-pound horse but helmets do balance the odds a bit.

Statistically, western riders are the hold out group. The most common argument has to do with a Western heritage. That western hat habit is about two hundred years old, a decent period of time as habits come and go. Dressage is about two thousand years old, and most of us consider Xenophon the founder, riding and writing about it in 406 BC. If dressage riders can wear helmets after centuries without them, it should be possible for Western riders to at least give it a try when riding.

Maybe you are rocking the backyard cowgirl image. Maybe you think your heritage, (and mine by the way), is so patriotic and pure that gravity doesn't work on you. I notice you defend it…well, defensively.

It isn't that I don't remember being a kid riding bareback in cut-offs. I still see online photos of girls like I was back then, smiling in the sun on a kid-broke horse. Only the byline is asking for prayers; she's in a coma. Or a photo of a little boy who loves rodeo but needs donations for medical bills after his horse fell on him. Someone usually comments, "Where's his helmet?" but it's painfully too late and almost seems mean to mention by then. Is his mom comforted remembering that she didn't wear a helmet as a kid?

Disclaimer: I am an equine professional. I read the small print when I buy liability insurance that says I'm responsible for the safety of others. Being knowledgeable about safety is part of my job and I would require helmets for my riders, even if my insurance didn't already. Are you the sort who hates laws put on personal freedom? We wouldn't need them if we all showed more personal responsibility. And this is the conversation that gets people defensive.

I know I can't change the minds of cowboys and cowgirls who think their proud heritage will save them from brain injury. Riders who think a fashion statement is more important than… okay, the rant begins again. Sorry. I'll take a breath…

Because there is no debate, nothing to defend. Helmets save lives, just like seat belts. And still, we needed the law. So there are helmet laws in a couple of states. The USEF has passed wide sweeping helmet requirements. Excuses are flimsy in the face of brain damage but years later, the resistance is still there. It seems hopeless. How many times does human ego get in the way of common sense in the horse world? Should we give up on these riders?

My *almost* bar fight was with a mother who had a concussion with memory loss and was still proudly bragging about riding without a helmet. Should a stranger be more concerned about her and her kids than she is? Will this bicker-fest ever change?

Then there's Hannah, our barn rat. She got a pink helmet for her second birthday and the rides started. Now she is almost big enough for the breeches that she wears under a purple sun dress or a princess costume. Her tiny paddock boots almost stay on her even tinier feet. The pink gloves are huge but they match her helmet, which does fit perfectly.

She climbs on top with her mom's help and calls, "Walk on!" Namaste, her horse, and I obey, and at the end of the ride, she always has a hug for him. She leans down and in a very quiet voice, she whispers, "I will love him forever."

Girls and horses: It is the oldest story in the world. With one pink improvement.

Dressage: Cackling at the Canter

In the 1980s, I marched with *Ladies Against Women*. Do you know the organization? They were a national group and there were two ways to join: You needed a permission note from your father, or a permission note from your husband. We marched in the Denver Do-Dah Parade, somewhere between the Lawn Chair Drill Team and the Basset Hound Rescue who had a dozen Bassets marginally harnessed and somewhat pulling an Iditarod dog sled. The *Ladies Against Women* carried signs with slogans like "I'd rather be ironing" and "59¢ is too much." One of us was pregnant *and* barefoot, and we all seemed a bit shocked being out of our kitchens.

Things were going well until someone took us seriously and threw their soda. My pink sponge rollers got all sticky. And to think that feminists have a reputation for having no sense of humor... Pshaw.

Now here I am a few decades later, again affiliated with a group rumored to have no sense of humor. I'm not sure where Dressage got its stodgy reputation. Is it our age? We have been around for a very long time, being the mother of so many other riding disciplines. Is it that silly shadbelly coat and white breeches? It's just tradition. I think you western riders understand that, taking so much pride in your hats the way you do. Besides, any rider who wears white obviously has a sense of humor.

In a way, a sense of humor is in our bylaws. The foundation

of our Dressage Training Pyramid requires the horse to be working through it's back freely, relaxed and forward. Some riders read the small print differently, but we begin horses with the premise that a horse must be physically and mentally free from tension or constraint in order to use itself to the fullest. It's funny, in a slightly perverse way, to think this fluid and free movement under saddle—liberty quality movement—is a starting point. It's just one of the dark charms of dressage. Are you laughing yet?

Relaxed + Forward = Happy horse. It's a result you can't get by fighting or intimidating your partner. If the horse needs relaxation, then the rider has to display it first. We carry all of our emotions in our bodies; in a sense we cue with our emotions. The horse hears the rider's feelings louder than the actual cue most of the time. The best riding position in the world can't make up for negative emotions in the saddle.

Are you in a perfection death spiral? The harder you try, the worse it gets; the more you want it, the harder you push; the harder you push, the more he resists. By now your sit bones are driving into your horse's back like a cinder block and no kind of expensive saddle pad will lessen the pain. Your horse thinks you are a humorless asshat. (Doesn't that word make you smile?)

Be deadly serious about your riding. There is no denying how much it matters to all of us. But discipline yourself to laugh it off; find a way to ride with a light heart. If you want to control something, start with your emotions. Don't do it for the judge or your trainer. Do it for your horse, because a happy seat in the saddle feels better to him. Period. There is no better reason.

Riding appears effortless when we relax and ride like we don't care. Yes, it's a lie, we all care too much. That's the point. Spare your horse your elite riding dreams and play instead. Laugh your way to advanced movements. Yes, it's counter-intuitive, but riding is supposed to be fun, remember?

The reason we need to be serious about having a sense of humor should be obvious by now. You can't force a horse to relax. Trying to force anything around a horse doesn't work and makes you look like a jerk. Then the doorway to good work shrinks to the size of an eye of a needle. You can't kick your way through that. You are on a very slippery slope here and it's your job to lead your horse to a better place. Yes, it takes patience and time to train a horse. But a sense of humor does make time pass more quickly.

Let your horse volunteer his best work, lightly and freely. Asked for by a light, happy seat and rewarded with a genuine smile and praise from the heart. *Good Boy.* Even if it's not perfect, it's a step in the right direction. Show your horse some praise and see what he returns to you.

While we are training them, our horses are training us right back. They teach us about humility first; humor makes that lesson easier to swallow.

The truth is to succeed at anything involving a horse you need a lightness of heart. Our passion for riding is deadly cruel without it. But serious isn't the same as stodgy. Focused isn't the same as dull. Most of all, forced isn't the same as volunteered. Be deadly serious about riding, but do it with a chuckle and a guffaw. If nothing else, people will think you're crazy and you'll get more private arena time.

Crank up the music. None of the stodgy classical stuff—let your horse pick something out of your comfort zone on the AM dial. Find that saddle pad with the ducks on it and get out the rainbow leg wraps. Let out a howling whoop when you get that extended trot or cackle like a chicken at the canter. Wear a happy face on your full seat breeches and be a member of the *Laughing Seat Riding Society.* Your horse will write the permission note.

Lighten up, this is dressage!

Listen First, Train Later

The first time I met him, he was two months old, standing in a stall with his mom. He was bright and intuitive, an Andalusian/ Appendix cross and soon-to-be my fiftieth birthday present to me.

We did it all right. I worked with him lightly over the next months and we got to know each other. The breeder did a slow-motion weaning process that was less stressful. We took our time and prepared ahead. I was actually aware that over sixty percent of foals develop ulcers when they are weaned.

When the day actually came for the colt to travel to my barn, I hauled a peaceful gelding up to keep him company in the trailer. We arrived early in the day, did a quiet job of loading the colt and took an uneventful hour drive back to my home barn.

The colt made friends with a donkey first, but everyone liked him and there was no drama. We spent the first afternoon exploring, friends dropped by, and he got hay snacks through the day. Everything was perfect.

That night I called the breeder to let her know we had arrived safely and settled in. I praised the colt for being brave and managing the day so well. I told her I was surprised to see him be so food aggressive at dinner-time and she said that was odd, he hadn't been that way in the past. We both did a phone shrug and I thanked her again.

The next morning I set about training some table manners. I asked him to step back and he pinned his ears, and we worked from there. He was a very smart horse who learned quickly. In no time at all, he was much less intimidating around hay and I was feeling great about my training skills. That was just the first time I didn't listen to this colt.

This is going to sound very obvious, but still, here goes: Horses don't speak English. They speak Horse. As the *theoretically* more advanced species, it's up to us to learn their language. The primary way they have to communicate with us is through their behavior. If we judge every behavior as bad or a training issue, we aren't listening to what they are actually trying to communicate as well as we could. My new colt told me in the clearest way he could that food hurt his stomach, that he was in pain; but regrettably, I trained that symptom away.

And just as obvious, training away a symptom is not the same thing as healing it. It doesn't address the actual problem so it will pop up again as another behavior and the miscommunication plants a seed of mutual confusion or maybe even distrust. Everyone tells me that their biggest goal is to have a better relationship with their horse. The best body position in the world will never take the place of a good ear.

Just to be clear, it is never okay with me for a horse to have bad ground manners and be dangerous, even if they are in pain. Part of the art of training is finding a balance of respect and honesty. If that's working, a horse shouldn't have to fight to be heard. If we listen to his small voice, or even just acknowledge it, he begins to trust us. And conversely, if we discipline a horse every time he tries to tell us something, he will shut down or go nuts. Just like we do in real life.

Think of being with horses as a game of charades. Their team is up and instead of categories like movies or book titles, they act out a behavior for us to guess the meaning. It might be a limp or excessive spookiness, or head tossing. We check for physical causes, then emotional ones. If we are brutally self-honest, we check to see if our horse is mirroring our own fears or anxiety. It's confusing and our perception might be challenged. That's why training is an art, remember?

"The opposite of art is not ugliness, it's indifference." —Elie Wiesel

Once you have listened to the message, then by all means, train away. Positive training is a calming gift. It is a way for a horse to find peace, a way he can know where he belongs in a chaotic world.

Too many times, we identify our horses as having bad human habits: "He is just being lazy." "He's crazy, he's seen that a million times." "He's a nervous Nelly, he just wants to run all the time."

Our first imperative in working with horses is always their well-being. Horses live in the moment and their reality is physically sensed through their bodies. Good riders calm their own brain chatter and get present in the moment. We will get better results if we listen with an open mind and not just treat our horses like badly behaved boyfriends.

The gift that comes with bad behavior is a chance for positive leadership. It's a chance to reward his vulnerability and honesty with compassion rather than punishment. Lots of us didn't grow up in homes that ran by these rules, and the help we give our horses heals us a bit as well.

You Be the Judge

"Too bad about that half pass to the left." My horse and I were leaving the arena after my test, reins long and my trademark competition smile: Lips stuck on my gums above my teeth. I had a great horse. The comment was made by a woman who felt no sympathy at all for that less-than-flawless half pass. We weren't friends really but she smiled. She might not have shoved herself through the hoops required to show her own horse and open herself up to the judgment of others, but she wanted me to know she was capable of recognizing wrong when she saw it.

The first year I showed, when my horse spooked at the letters and ran off with me in each test, she never passed a word my way. But now our hard work was paying off and as we advanced, she developed the habit of letting me know our shortcomings from her enlightened position on the rail. She still didn't show because she could never find a horse good enough.

No hard feelings; I was living my dream. I wanted to be here in the arena since watching the rich kids in 4-H at the county fair. It was before I knew there were kids even richer than those kids.

Some riders say they hate the show world, that all competition is wicked and evil. They will never show. Fair enough, it isn't for everyone. The rant still rings of judgment. Reminder: Pre-judging isn't the same thing as *not* judging.

Besides, you can be just as judgmental and not even have to

leave the house. It's open season on riding videos on YouTube. We have free speech and anyone can comment. If we aren't face to face, is there any reason to hold your tongue? Threaten bodily harm if you want. The truth is that even if we didn't have horses, we would be still judging other people's appearance, intelligence, lifestyle. It's human nature to notice. It's how we learn and grow our perceptions. Most of all, in the process of judging others, we judge ourselves. Maybe it's the need to label things as right or wrong that is the most damaging.

Disclaimer: I'm no angel. I have all kinds of judgment. It's judgment that I even remember this woman's comment from the rail twenty years ago. Beyond that, my work is about judgment. Giving a riding lesson begins with an assessment of a horse and rider, balancing clarity and honesty with as much understanding and kindness as possible. It would be easier to yell and name-call but I've had lessons like that and I notice I didn't learn much.

Competing your horse is about being your best self when it matters. It's hard. It takes discipline. It builds character. Maybe the best reason to show is that it changes the view from the rail. It changes who you are with your horse and it gives you a chance to change your view of others. Is re-compassionize a word?

There's an old adage—if you can't say something nice, don't say anything at all. I go with that only if you are in such a rage that your eye is twitching and you spit when you speak. Short of that level of anger, I disagree. It makes us passive-aggressive and we languish, lifting ourselves up by standing on others.

Yes, this is a parable. There are bigger things in the world than showing horses. It's been a mean summer, stressful with lots of challenge and loss. And entirely too many harsh arm-chair judgments on anyone or anything that falls short, touted by pundits who have nothing on the line. It makes me tired. It will always be easier to shoot down someone else than find the strength to stand up and be vulnerable.

My first riding mentor was also a judge, and she was very

clear. She said it was a cheap shot to look for faults. Any idiot could pick them out; it took no special perception to tell which horse was struggling. In the end, you would be left mitigating failures and giving the blue ribbon to the least bad. She encouraged me to look for what I liked and affirm that. Judge the best in the ride, let your eye rest there and ignore everything else.

In the end, being critical of others makes us earthbound with self-loathing judgment, thinly veiled in our criticism of others. And focusing on the worst just breeds more. How does that feel? Maybe it's time to sit up straight.

Judgment is really a vote of how you see the world; how you want the world to be. The most votes win and you can vote as often as you like. Consider what's at stake. Sometimes in the dark, rising up and casting an unlikely vote can change everything.

Consistency:
Doing Math in the Saddle

Consistency is a great aid but do you know how it actually works? There's an analogy I heard decades ago that has stuck with me. It involves bank accounts. You're right; never listen to me about money, but it's not that kind of bank account.

Start by thinking that you and your horse each have a bank account of experience. For your horse it's a reckoning of all of his experiences with humans–all the good times and all those times where he got scared and had no help. Confidence, fear, willingness to partner, and what caused pain and when rewards were given. The account is his possession. He's the one who quantifies the contents.

Your account has all of your horsemanship experiences, including the times you were confident or fearful. It's what you have learned from experts and how well you listen to your horse. You get extra points for patience. A tiny corner is reserved for your dreams. It's your personal wealth as a potential partner for a horse.

It's simple. In any situation, either of you can make deposits or withdrawals. An experienced rider can help a young horse with a deposit of patience and positive training. An old campaigner can enrich a novice rider by carrying them through a rough spot. Sometimes it's referred to as the Twenty Year Rule; for the best results the sum of experience shared by the horse and rider should equal twenty years or so.

It makes perfect sense; all of us are the sum of our experience. But there was one problem. Back then, I had a very green and spooky young horse and I wasn't as brave and crazy as when I was a kid. Bankrupt. Neither of us had much to draw on. We had good intentions but it was an against-the-odds start.

It's a pretty common dilemma. Most rideable horses that end up in rescue have training problems, stemming from poor handling. Some riders manage to buy a well-trained horse, but without the right skills, the horse's account is quickly depleted and he becomes resistant and sour. A rider's good intentions can become spent on a confused horse, as well.

Seen this way, it's a fair, impartial accounting of any situation, whether it's a competition horse or a trail horse. Seeing a horse/rider problem as a math equation takes some of the emotion and blame out of it on both sides and that's a great first step. Guilt and failure are negative deposits.

Start now. The past is data; you can't change that, so let it be. Horses have strong memories and if that trait is working against you, your best hope is to layer good memories on top that will eventually out-number the bad. You have to get the numbers in his favor. If your confidence is shaky, or you need a few more training tools, then make that investment in getting good, professional help and watch your own numbers go up.

Here is where consistency comes in. Horses love a routine and it's the sacred job of every rider to leave the horse in a better place at the end of the ride than the beginning. It's our version of *First Do No Harm*.

Just like the stock market, horses are always moving in an overall tendency. They are getting better or worse. Long range investments have less drama and are more dependable, while others think taking their life savings to Vegas for the weekend is a smart bet. It's a choice.

Start your ride start slowly with a warm-up that relaxes and supples him. Reward him for being alive. Get happy. Notice him liking what you're saying; reward that. On this one day, the most you can do is have one ride. Lower your expectations of perfecting your world in an instant. Instead of getting greedy, be content to make one good deposit.

The truest thing that I know about horses is that it's time and consistency that trains a horse. There are no shortcuts, no get rich quick schemes, that will ever take the place of a simple Piggy Bank approach.

The thing we pay attention to grows. If we make a problem bigger than it is by isolating it and scrutinizing it into a huge issue, then we squander an opportunity. We can invest worry until the issue blocks out the daylight or invest in knowing it all works out in hindsight. Because it really does.

Here's the secret: never give up. Get a tortoise tattoo if you need to, but just stick it out, slowly and patiently, because consistency is the greatest kindness a horse will ever know. He wants the confidence to clearly understand where he should be, without fear of pain. One positive ride at a time, consistency will buy you a new normal.

You know that rider that you see who is smiling, riding a dream horse that will do anything? That horse people call a push-button horse? They focused on what was right about their ride and built their fortune one penny at a time. It was no accident; it was a long-term goal. Praise their consistency.

And then one day, if you are very, very lucky, you will take a short twenty-minute ride on a green and frightened horse. In those moments you will have a wealth of understanding and positive leadership to give him. You will be an aid to him. Then he will exhale that first shallow blow of baby trust, as you exhale a breath rich in the memory of that first horse you invested your best self in. Rich in the knowledge that you have something of value to offer a horse.

Breath, the Miracle Cue

It might be the simplest cue to execute, as well as the last one we think to use. I know it's the cue that does the most good. And it's certainly the cue that's the most natural: Breathe.

Alas, it's also the cue most under-rated. I see riders disregard the suggestion immediately. It's like they want a real tool that works every time, not some airy-fairy imaginary, breath-y thing. They want a magic body position or a leg aid that gets dramatic results, like a spur with an electric cattle prod attachment... only kinder and more compassionate. Something that commands respect and undeniable leadership, not some puny suggestion to just breathe. Such an insignificant suggestion barely warrants a try.

Well, not to horses. Breath is the universal animal language. It's the initial tell-all greeting between animals. They size us up by the way we breathe and the emotions carried in our breath. It is a major part of leadership, communication, and relaxation in the herd. We are prone to diminish the horse's behavior from taking intuitive stock of who we are to them begging for a treat. But then our sense of smell usually doesn't even point out manure before we step in it. However we try to depreciate their greeting, they sense so much more about us than what we had for lunch.

When our breath is shallow, our chest is inhibited and tight, sometimes even concave, with a tight jaw and tense eyes. It sends a message of restriction, fear, resistance. Our movements can even seem coyote-like in a stalking, nervous way. Clearly we not leadership material.

A change in breathing is the very first message a horse sends his rider that things aren't okay. When we see a horse taking shallow breaths, we know he's tense. That's our cue; we seize up to a flat, shallow breath ourselves. The horse feels that concern and as a prey animal, and looks for the source of trouble. Then his poll gets tense in the process and his oxygen intake is impacted. His head comes up and our shoulders get tight in response, along with our hands on the reins. He feels restriction on his bit, and now he's sure there is a problem, so he loses forward, which is exactly like losing confidence. Then the rider either gets more tense or more adversarial.

You can see where the ride is headed by now, right? There are a million outcomes from here, but it all started with breath. Breathing was the first cue and it doesn't matter who started it, good or bad, the horse or the rider. In the end, the mood was set and the leadership defined in the first few seconds by breathing.

But if we do manage to breathe, our chests expand and our vertebrae re-align. Muscles soften, jaws relax. Elbows unlock and legs get long and soft. Oxygen gets to our brains and we think more clearly. Communication is calm, responses acknowledged. Our body cues softness and rhythm. A horse will follow us on this ride too.

Breath shared with a horse is an actual, literal cue either to relax or come apart. Now is it worth paying attention to?

"Breath is the bridge which connects life to consciousness, which unites your body to your thoughts. Whenever your mind becomes scattered, use your breath as the means to take hold of your mind again."
⊠ Thích Nhất Hạnh

Uh-huh. Breathing is also the thing that can bring a horse back. If your brain panicked or lost focus, if you notice that things have sped up—and you're being more reactive than pro-active—and the clock ticking is getting louder, faster, and things are a bit out of control... Slow it all down with your breath. Whether your mind has an anxiety runaway or it just wanders away from your horse to those pesky thoughts of self-doubt or frustration or what a lousy day you had at work, shut all that negative chatter down with a breath, just a disciplined breath.

Yes, they make drugs for that. Breathing seems like a lame suggestion in the face of the pharmaceutical universe, in the face of a training disaster or world angst. It can even seem insignificant standing next to a horse. That doesn't make it any less of a miracle.

I like one-two-three breathing. It's simple. Count to three on an inhale, let the air inflate your ribs in all directions, let it rest in the bottom of your belly for a count. Then exhale slowly and count to three. Do it in rhythm with your horse's stride. Breathe into all the tight spots, up to your eye-brows and down to your ankles. Breathe into your horse's spine, to the tip of his tail, into his very heart.

Perhaps you've noticed that talking to yourself about being in the moment with your horse isn't the same thing as authentically being *in the moment*. Breath is the how-to aid, the thing that fills the gap between thought and reality. I have never met a horse that didn't respond. Learn to be aware of your breathing so you can have a better ride with your horse, and let your blood pressure benefit as well.

All bad things for a horse happen with a loss of rhythm: Spooking, bucking, bolting. All good things for a horse happen rhythmically: Trotting, grazing, breathing. And when they relax, they give a big blow from deep inside. We can learn it from them.

Drop your shoulders and let go. Breathe deep, expand those ribs to give your generous heart room, then exhale peace. Inhale. What if we stopped fighting ourselves and suppleness became our greatest strength? Exhale. A deep breath is an act of confidence in itself.

It isn't the least you can do, it's the very most. Keep breathing.

Being Grateful for Things You Don't Like

My favorite training mentor had a habit that drove me nuts. She would be working with a horse who spooked or flipped his head or had some other issue that made him a disaster and when she climbed on, if you were close, you could hear her say in a low and quiet voice, "Goody, goody." She would have a small smile and be cheerful.

The woman was nuts. It was like she couldn't tell right from wrong. She loved a bad ride. It wasn't that she wanted the adrenaline thrill of trying to stay on, and she didn't pick fights. She just thought a conversation with a horse got more interesting once some resistance showed up.

I was a novice rider just beginning to compete a young horse and neither of us was very confident. One of us was trying way too hard. And it was so important that he was perfect. We hated problems. Okay it was me, I hated it when he was bad.

So I was a conditional rider. I did well if my horse was confident and in a good mood, but if something went sideways, I couldn't cope. I didn't act out and jerk on his mouth or use a whip. Instead I got quietly resistant. Every cue started with the disciplinary word *don't*. Don't spook, don't run off, don't quit. If I could just try to control his every breath, just not allow him to come apart... I was totally focused on resisting my horse's resistance.

So naturally, my trainer ruined my Zen by celebrating the bad like she did.

Let me be clear: She was right. I was wrong and being a judgmental jerk, the kind of person who discriminates against imperfection. The kind of person that I don't like much.

There is a tiny moment wedged right between the point where everything is going well and you love your ride, and that point where both you and your horse start to come apart. This tiny moment is when we stop listening and start ordering. And when a confused or frightened horse gets told that he's wrong. Understanding gets sacrificed for external appearances. We become bullies, jerking and kicking, or just holding on for dear life. We become part of the problem.

But in that tiny moment, when you just start to feel him tense, you have a choice. You don't have to flinch and take the bait. In that tiny moment, you could confound nay-sayers and defy common sense and choose to get happy. What possible good can come out of making your horse wrong?

Instead, you can take a breath and discipline *yourself*. You can do something totally crazy. You can smile and let your hands breathe out some reins. You can embrace the moment, leave the criticizing to others, and get on about helping your horse. Less correction, more direction.

Amazingly, in that same tiny moment, he is right there wanting to hear from you. Horses live in the present and because horses don't get stuck using right or wrong labels, they are more fluid. Their minds are capable of change, at least to the degree their rider's are. In that instant you can turn things around with a pat. You can change who you are and how your horse responds.

I rode with this genius trainer for five years. I learned some fancy party tricks and by the end, people thought I had a great horse. The truth was even better than that, but first I had to learn to see my horse as perfect and willing, especially when appearances were deceiving. I held to that truth and it made all the difference.

I am exceedingly grateful for horses in my life, but even more than that, I am grateful for this bit of knowledge, passed down from my mentor. It's enough to make you laugh at its simplicity—this awareness that it's all good, if you approach it that way.

Too Pollyanna-ish for you? It's true there are some big ugly issues in the horse world, like slaughter and abuse. Things so nasty that it's easier to look away and ignore them. It can take some strength to look that kind of darkness in the face and not flinch. To take a breath and start to work on a positive solution. My perfect horses taught me that keeping an open mind and expecting the best beats name-calling and whining about what is wrong–Every. Single. Time.

"My horse has a problem with his canter depart." "You can't save them all."

Now I'm the trainer and with a nod to my mentor, I say, "Goody, goody." Because I know the one the rider thinks has the problem, is not really the one with the problem at all. Because this is a chance for something good to happen.

Vet Visit! Breathing is Connection

Emergency vet call! One of my boarder's horses is sick. He's a draft cross, timid but kind. He likes things to move in horse time. When the vet and his tech arrived, they hurried into his run. He remembers vets and tries to be good, but needles scare him. Intruders moving fast scare him. By moving fast, I mean at a normal walk.

The tech was new; she didn't know us here. She immediately took a firm hold on the lead rope. No one around here holds a rope tight. It can cue a horse to pull back. "He'll be fine, go slow," I say. She flashes me the *"I'm a professional"* look. That's fair.

So by now, the horse's eyes are wide and he is a bit taller than his usual 17 hands—tense and barely breathing. And the vet is taking vital signs as the tech tries to stabilize his huge head. The horse is slightly alarmed; he's used to doing that himself.

Disclaimer: I love vet techs. I've done a bit of time in her shoes. It's hard work with miserable hours, and job one is to manage the horse in such a way that the vet is safe. No one wants techs or vets injured and sick horses are not predictable. To tell the truth, lots of the horses they work on are dangerous because of little or no training. It's a very challenging job and I appreciate her.

So the tech grips the lead rope right at the clip and is holding fast. The horse is resisting her resistance—the fight is all right there. And one other small detail: The circumference of his neck is twice her waist size. This isn't a fair fight—he could launch her over the top of the barn.

She is facing the horse's hind, toward the vet, who's prepping an injection now. The good horse is wide-eyed and electric. This makes the vet a bit tense; he's probably remembering this horse in the past. The tech trying to do her best, responds by taking an even tighter hold on the horse. She's not quite on her tip-toes yet.

I am standing about three feet in front of the horse, behind the tech's back. I take a deep breath through my open mouth, counting to three silently. I hold it an instant and then exhale it through my mouth, slow and audible like a sigh—again counting one-two-three. In the middle of this breath, the tech glances over her shoulder at me with brows furrowed. Like I'm crazy or something. I bet she runs into a lot of weird gray-haired women in her day, so I give her the benefit of the doubt and smile mid-exhale.

Breath is how we all connect, but especially horses. It's just that simple.

I take a second deep slow inhale and this time the tech doesn't glance at me, the vet is close to giving the shot but seems to have paused.

(As I'm writing this, the thought crosses my mind that I yammer on about breathing in every essay I write, in every riding lesson I give. Even as the words are in the air, I can see the rider blowing me off. She wants a real cue that will make a difference. Not some bliss-ninny suggestion to breathe. Readers probably do the same.)

As I began my third deep breath, the horse dropped his head like a rock. And by drop his head, I mean twelve or eighteen inches. The vet tech turned, looked at me full on like I stole the cake, and began reconsidering gray-haired women. The vet gave the shot with almost no one noticing, finishing the syringe with the end of my exhale.

I'm no genius; it's common sense. If breathing is the most

important thing in the saddle, *and it is*, then it must be twice that important during stress on the ground. It's an anchor for a horse under sedation, essential for a horse in a bit of shock from an injury, and I believe it absolutely saves lives during a colic. Breathing is one of those things that is its own reward. Meaning as you are breathing for your horse, deep to the bottom of your lungs, it is the anti-panic drug for you, too. And you need to be calm for your horse. He doesn't want to hear you hysterically shrieking, either out loud or inside your mind. It never helps. Sure, it's hard to see a horse in pain. We might be stuck on the spot, but even if we can't move our feet, we can be strong in our breath.

The meaning of breath is much deeper than words. The thread of his life began with a first inhale and his dam and herd answered him. So, we share our horse/human breath back and forth every day, in ancient horse language, to let him know he is safe.

And if you are very lucky, if you are the very best partner, when the time comes to say goodbye, you can help him. In that precious moment you can breathe with him, the same breath you shared in a lifetime of laughter and tears and warm sun on his neck. There is no finer salute for a good horse than to share that last breath. Because just like all the other times, breath is how we connect.

The Everyday Value of Dressage

Is your horse a different person under-saddle?

Maybe tacking up is all good, but once you are ready to mount, he dances around a bit. But you're athletic enough to grab on and swing a leg over, pulling on the reins to slow him down. Oh well, then his head comes up, but you're no pansy. Sure, his trot is jolting and his neck counter-bent, but you can ride him through it. So he's trotting hollow but you can just pull down and back on the reins to fix it. Now he's braced as much as you are and the trot is really rough. It's so uncomfortable to ride, that you move him to the canter. After all, you're a *committed* rider, so you just push through it. And then, because it's your intention to progress in your riding and not be at Training Level forever, you try a shoulder-in by pulling the inside rein and twisting him to a tense, hoof-dragging crawl. And maybe forty-five minutes later, you get a bit of softness. Partly because you are exhausted and fighting less, and he's taking the cue. You cool him out, give him lots of treats, and the next ride starts the same way.

Maybe you don't notice you're being adversarial at all. Maybe this kind of riding feels normal or even necessary to you. You know you're being rougher than you want to be, but your particular horse requires it. It's just who he is. *You're wrong.* Maybe a trainer has told you that there is some dominance fight that you have to win by force, so your horse will respect you. Or some nonsense about not releasing until your horse does. (I am about to be very unpopular.) But *they're wrong,* too.

You can't reprimand a horse into happy work anymore than a man can dominate a woman into love. Fear doesn't inspire horses any more than it does us. If a horse's walk is tense and not rhythmic, that isn't going to improve much at the trot. And if the trot is tense and hollow, then to be honest, his intimidated canter will be painful for all involved.

"For what the horse does under compulsion...is done without understanding; and there is no beauty in it either, any more than if one should whip and spur a dancer." —Xenophon, 430 B.C. (My all-time favorite quote; no one has said it better in the last twenty-four and a half centuries.)

The ride you are getting right now is no accident—that's good news. The two of you can improve, but the rider has to be different before the horse can be. I repeat, you have to change first.

There's no better time than the present to go back to basics and peel back another layer of understanding. When you see a more advanced rider it just means they have gone back to the beginning more times than you. Not so glamorous when you look at it that way, but nothing else about riding is glamorous, so here we are... all of us at the beginning together. Let's walk.

Dressage training is built on a foundation that says—first and always—a horse must be relaxed and forward. That is square one; as true for Intro Level as Grand Prix. The small print says that we may not sacrifice forward movement for relaxation, and even more challenging, we may not sacrifice supple relaxation for forward movement. This is why dressage judges have as many words for *hollow and tense* as Eskimos do for snow.

Reminder: We don't actually ride this way to please judges. We do it for the well-being of the horse. This foundation is my favorite thing about dressage. It's a simple, and not at all easy, path to partnership if we persevere and listen. We can't make a horse relax with a cue like a down-stay. Training relaxation requires a relationship where the language is more evolved than

"Me—Tarzan, You—Jane." This is where I remind you yet again that riding is an art.

After this seemingly airy-fairy chat, do you want some practical advice? There is nothing more important than a good warm-up. It sets the tone for the ride. If you are riding a young, sound horse, it takes twenty minutes for the synovial fluid to warm in his joints and be ready for work. Give your horse time. By the way, your joint fluid isn't any faster.

The secret to success with a horse is not mystical, it's fundamental. How your horse is moving is always more important than what he is actually doing. It can take a long time to understand this. Riders want to race ahead to the party tricks: flying changes or lateral work or piaffe. Those movements require an even more artful balance of relaxed and forward, with a profound and practical embrace of the fundamentals.

In other words, go slow. It's like a pass/fail test. If your horse is tense, everything lacks rhythm and is a fight. But with the freedom of forward movement, balanced with relaxation, training anything gets easy and puts both of you on the same side. The miracle of dressage is that to do it correctly, we have to evolve beyond domineering control. Ta-da; partners!

A horrible generalization: I sometimes think that the reason women compete so successfully in dressage is that we partner with horses naturally, partly because we share an understanding of the down-side of dominance. We don't enjoy being told what to do either. Just an observation.

The Stepford Horses,
Dominated to Submission

Remember the *Stepford Wives*—a little too submissive, a little too darkly docile? I saw horses just like them last week and I'm still in a snit. They were at a riding facility; a group lesson of fairly novice western riders. Each of the horses had a shank bit, each of the riders used spurs. The horses moved like the zombie-wives who had lost the will to live... altered into submission by their self-important husbands. If one of the horses did lift his head to see where he was going, there was a hard bump on the bit, metal on bone, painful enough to shut down or kill forward movement in any horse. That's where the spurs came in. (There is also a dressage version of this, of course.)

If you think domination is good horsemanship, you're wrong. Seeing your horse cower underneath you is ugly.

I'm preaching to the choir. If you read this blog, I doubt you ride this way. My actual clients, who always think I'm talking about them, all know for a fact this isn't them. I'm not accusing any of you of being this kind of brutal, soul-killing rider. Still, balance and forward can always improve, and in an attempt to relieve the PTSD burned onto my eyeballs, can we talk about balance and willingness?

Let's compare riding a horse to driving a car. It's a lousy, demeaning comparison because even though some horses are expected to perform mechanically, in truth, riding is an art involving lightness and partnership with an animal of intellect and emotion. Not like cars at all.

To begin, a horse has a drive-line at the girth area. In other words, where the rider/driver sits in the saddle. All energy to move ahead comes from behind the drive-line, so the hind-end is the engine/gas pedal, and in front of the girth is where the brake is.

Forward movement is the finest virtue a horse can have; the ability to cover ground in a rhythmic and relaxed way. It begins with the horse's soft, strong hind leg stepping under to push forward, allowing the energy to flow softly over his back, through his withers and his poll, and landing sweetly on his lips. The result of this push from behind is that the horse's poll is soft and his head on the vertical, like horses moving at liberty. It's a rider's goal to recreate that relaxed liberty sort of energy; to let it flow sweetly, passing through the rider in the saddle––at any gait.

That's the idea, but if the poll is tense everything changes. There's a delicate front-to-back balance crucial to the horse. To the degree that the rider creates tension in front, or lays on the brake, forward is impeded because forward isn't defined by the speed the horse is moving, but instead the horse's effective, flexible use of his body. Just as you wouldn't drive using the gas and brake simultaneously. Just as you couldn't run easily in a cinched-up back brace.

Still, we land in the saddle and immediately bump the horse's nose down, or use a rein to pull his head to the side before the first step. Some trainers do it, but it isn't any more effective than turning the steering wheel when the car is parked. Using the hand brake, meaning the inside rein, before the horse is even moving, makes a horse lose balance and rhythm—even at the halt. What could have been a dance, ends up in a bar brawl. And I might be ranting about those Stepford horses again.

A good rider always has more energy from behind (gas) than restriction in the front (brakes) but it's a fine balance. We move off at a walk, engaging our seat and legs and letting the reins rest. In dressage we want the horse moving forward to the bit, in support of his natural balance, roundness, and flexibility at the poll. It takes finesse, lightness, and sheer will to stay out of his way.

Most of us unbalance our horses when learning. It's our nature to pull on the reins for control or an impression of the desired silhouette. So we cue stop and go simultaneously, confusing the horse by grabbing his bit and spurring him forward. Or soft hands can flow with the horse's movement, creating no resistance and getting none in return. Hands can ride the brake every stride, or rest lightly on the wheel, careful to not over-correct. Hands are the aid we should use least while riding.

How can you tell if you ride the brake, being too restrictive with the reins? That is *so* simple—your horse tells you. He's tense and upside down. He flips his head or tries to pull the reins out of your hand. It isn't disobedience, he's letting you know by sending your resistance right back to you. It's what happens when you tap the brake--the ride gets jerky. You can choose to take the cue gratefully and continue the conversation; you can be as responsive as you want your horse to be. Or you can shout him down and punish him when he asks for kindness.

If the excuse/thought crosses your mind that you need a stronger bit, please reconsider. A stronger aid will not help your hands and they are how you got here in the first place. A bit that is more cruel is the worst thing you can do.

The saddest thing about fearful Stepford horses is that they are silenced, never to waltz, or sing into their rider's ear. By correcting the horse before he's had a chance to volunteer, the ride becomes flat and two-dimensional. As hard as it is on the horse, it's the rider that loses the most.

An Equine Cure for a
Type-A Personality

First, consider the horse. He is a majestic, elegant animal with a free spirit—intelligent, playful, and spontaneous. He is nothing short of awe-inspiring. He canters over the earth with his muscles rippling and his tail flagged, drinking the wind like cool water. He has been the very image of freedom and beauty since the beginning of time.

Now consider the Type-A rider. Psychologist Saul McLeod writes, *"Type A individuals tend to be very competitive and self-critical. They strive toward goals without feeling a sense of joy in their efforts or accomplishments. Inter-related with this is the presence of a significant life imbalance. This is characterized by a high work involvement. Type A individuals are easily 'wound up' and tend to overreact. They also tend to have high blood pressure (hypertension)."*

"Type A personalities experience a constant sense of urgency: Type A people seem to be in a constant struggle against the clock. Often, they quickly become impatient with delays and unproductive time, schedule commitments too tightly, and try to do more than one thing at a time, such as reading while eating or watching television."

And he continues, *"Type A individuals tend to be easily aroused to anger or hostility, which they may or may not express overtly. Such individuals tend to see the worse in others, displaying anger, envy and a lack of compassion. When this behavior is expressed overtly (i.e. physical behavior) it generally involves aggression and possible bullying."*

That seems a little harsh. And gratuitous. Maybe even mean. As a *recovering* Type A individual, I notice a lot of us are impatiently attracted to horses. We crave synchronicity with this beautiful, ethereal animal. They do say opposites attract, but that's just the beginning.

I'll use myself as a bad example. I was 25 years old and showing my one-of-a-kind work in the best fine art jewelry gallery in the country–on Fifth Avenue in New York City. And at home my baseboards were spotless.

Then I entered the twelve-step program for recovery, meaning I bought a horse. He was a brilliant weanling who I could mold perfectly, someone who would train me to exhale. Again and again, to the point of hyperventilating in the beginning.

There's a word left out of that long-winded Type A definition; the one word that hurts the most to admit: self-loathing. We push too hard to make up for our imperfections, yet we stay conscious of each one. We see them in our horses. A strategy to fake leadership can work to a point with some horses, if you are a big enough bully, or if art and beauty don't matter to you. I was out of luck on both counts. On the bright side, I didn't enjoy feeling like a loser either.

Type A riders like control a bit too much. Some of us control freaks micro-manage our horse's nose into being afraid to take a breath—before we clear the mounting block. Type A's and horses are kind of a perfect storm. The harder we try, the less we receive, the more we demand, the more resistant the horse becomes, the bigger the fight…but most of us internalize it stubbornly. Then if it's a really bad day, a giggling kid rides by bareback and mocks all your work. But Type A's are not quitters, so we double down.

Then, if we have a very good horse, he doubles down too, refusing to submit to soul-killing repetition and mind control.

He requires equality, the thing we doubt most about ourselves. We should have just gone to therapy in the first place because we can imagine a better way. We are haunted by beauty: some riders and horses have a synergy and together they ride just to the edge of control—and balance there, sharing perfection. There is brilliance in the art of the edge, but you have to give up some control to let the horse be there. You have to trust him. These are the moments that hook us forever because we become vulnerable partners. Our rules and restrictions fall away and in the moment, we are as authentic as a horse. It might happen doing flying changes in the arena or it might be picking a trail over uneven ground. It's humbling to feel your horse rise up under you and offer himself.

And if you feel it once, just an instant, the addiction takes hold and we try to re-create it at all cost. That desire is our doom and for a time, things get worse by our own force of will. Instead, like a surfer waiting for the perfect wave, we have to stay open and be ready to go along.

Our intention is to make perfection, but perfection is already a horse's natural state. Thinking that we need to micro-manage the horse is the ultimate vote of no trust. The more we hold our horse or correct the mistake before it happens, the more our horse loses confidence in his own ability. We damage his balance and rhythm but most of all, we stifle his personality and individuality. We end up damaging the traits we loved the most and progress is simply not possible—we've managed to get in our own way.

It takes a strange courage to un-control the outcome. Truth be told, Type A's aren't that into freedom and trust after all.

I'm lucky. My horses never had much tolerance for my intolerant ways. And since I was Type A, I controlled myself… to give them time to answer; time to be beautiful and intelligent. Hush. I had to quit nagging long enough to let him volunteer. Then I had to find my manners and let him know how I felt. It required honesty, in the moment, beyond external noise. I had to be real in order to progress.

The best reason to improve our riding is that it allows the horse to work his magic on us. The more we get out of his way, and let him carry himself, the more he gains the confidence to partner in our dance. Our riding should not limit the horse's best qualities but rather, encourage the horse to help us possess them also.

It's a perfect plan: Equine passion pulls us past the self-loathing part and then horses mentor us to wholeness. We can learn compassion where there used to be criticism, and baseboards be damned, so much more about ourselves to like.

Riding with Intention

Of course he knows what you're thinking. Does anyone think they can hide their feelings from their horse? Even for a minute?

A horse's physical awareness is so acute that they seem intuitive. Most of us think our horses are psychic because it's easier to believe than how limited our own senses are.

Compared to prey animals, we're slow-witted. Don't feel bad about it. We've got lots of skills. We have an intellect that can remember the past and dream of the future; we have the ability to reason and think creatively. We can daydream. Of course none of these mental skills are much help on top of a horse, who remains constantly awake in the moment. Meaning that knowing technique and communicating with the horse are two very different things. It's what makes marginal riders into opinionated rail-birds.

But we want to improve, so we read a book or twenty. Maybe we spend hours watching videos on YouTube, or investing in riding lessons. Meanwhile your horse is still in the present, sensing the environment. It's all he ever does. Prey animals stay alive that way, while we are comparing foreign accents and pondering which celebrity-designed training aid to try next.

The challenging part of riding is navigating the gap between intellectual knowledge and the ability to use it effectively. In other words, matching the thing felt in the saddle with the right learned response.

When I was first competing in dressage, I was riding a young

Arabian and he ran off with me in every test. He didn't leave the arena but it was ugly. Back at the trailer, my trainer would ask, "Couldn't you tell he was running off?"

Of course I could tell. It was a no-brainer—I couldn't post fast enough. In the moment that he started to speed up, I would pull up a mental list of possible corrections for that particular problem. Then I would go down my list once or twice and then narrow it down to a couple of options, but by then it didn't really matter which one I picked. It was too late. Time was way past for a small correction; now I had to just stay on till the next transition and hope it was a walk so I could pull myself together.

Think less, feel more: When I eventually found myself present in that first stride of the runaway, a light half-halt gave him the balance and confidence to stay with me. Simple.

One of the most dependable traits we have as riders in the beginning is that when we engage our brain, we stop physically riding. In the beginning, it's as if we can either think, or ride, but not do both simultaneously. Usually when the brain engages, the seat stops following. That's a halt cue.

Technical information about body position, proper use of the legs and contact with the reins is crucial in order to progress, but while your brain is busy assimilating this information, you can't abandon the horse you're riding.

All the technique in the world doesn't help you if it's applied poorly. Even if you have a good set of mental index cards, there's no time to find the one you're looking for quick enough in the saddle. And if all of that isn't enough, there's this one last wrench in the works: every horse is a bit different and the same cue doesn't work the same way. It's a horse; everything changes all the time.

But when you watch advanced riders, there is no time lag. It's as if thinking and feeling can happen simultaneously; as if they don't even need index cards. In order to bridge the gap between novice riding and advanced riding and improve our skills, we have to change how we approach them. In other words, the skills don't really change so much as our perception of them. There is no place for bigger and louder cues; this when the idea that *less is more* becomes most important. Advanced riders are more responsive, so their horses follow suit. I believe one of the biggest things a horse senses about us is our intent. It's the color that tints all the cues we give. If we are dominating or watching the clock, our intention takes on the color of a storm cloud and simple tasks like catching or trailering the horse become difficult. If you're positive and listening to your horse, it'll be a sunny, warm color. Too silly? Give it a try; it's harder than it sounds.

I would define a positive intention as similar to focus, but maybe a bit more open and accepting and less reactive or restrictive. This intention is the place your open mind stays poised, inside of every stride, not forcing a result but encouraging a tendency. It's the place that a horse comes to volunteer partnership. You'd hate to miss it while micro-managing a leg-yield and reciting a classical dressage quote.

Bridging the gap between intellectualizing and feeling means less trying and more listening. The strength involved is mental, so a little humility is a good idea. Schooling consistent intention will get you farther, faster than any book or video, because it's honest real-time information for your horse.

Talking down to a horse, whose perceptions are ahead of ours in the first place, is always a bad idea. The only way to keep up with him is to send a positive intention on ahead. It's the most crazy, counter-intuitive thing, except if you're a horse.

Tips for the Fat Rider (What?!)

Are you are just too fat to ride? Then go wait in your room.
Did that work? Did you actually go? Of course not. Can we stop this now?

I have a video a friend shot of my horse and me competing many years ago. Showing was challenging in the beginning but we progressed. This was a second or third level test, and things were really coming together.

I remember this video especially because my friend was reluctant to give my camera back to me and the reason became obvious. As my horse and I started the test, the first movement was an extended trot on the diagonal, and that was when I heard them. There were two unfamiliar voices recorded; they must have been standing next to the camera. The first voice mentions how bad she thinks I look in my show coat. The second voice agrees that we're unattractive—and that riders my size always look dumpy on a horse.

Next I hear my friend clear her throat loudly, twice, and then a small gasp. There was conspicuous silence for the rest of the test.

International competition is one thing, and amateurs showing at the local fairgrounds is another. For the record, I wasn't wild about my coat either but if you manage to get your horse past second level, you really have to focus on more than fashion. Too many times, women are their own worst enemies on the subject of self-image. We let extra weight betray us, or give us the right to betray other women. It's a cheap shot. Judge the ride, judge our understanding of dressage principles, but can we air-brush out superficial rail-birds?

Educated opinion advises that a rider and tack be about twenty percent of the horse's weight, give or take. This arbitrary number doesn't consider the horse's age or conformation, the type of riding being done, or the rider's balance and skill in the saddle.

Don't misunderstand. Nothing makes me crazier than seeing a grown man on a small pony or a rider so out of balance that the horse's stride is tense and uneven. At the same time, I've seen plenty of horses struggle with light riders as well. A horse/rider partnership is a bit more complicated than a math equation.

Serious obesity is a concern, but if you are killing yourself over twenty pounds, lighten up. I'm going to make an assumption now—since I've never in my life met a woman so pleased with her body that she was physically confident—and give some tips for over-weight riders. Yes, I would know.

First, feed your horse as you tack him up. Horses are grazers and create about two liters of stomach acid an hour, so he'll do better if he has something in his stomach. And watch your own blood sugar and keep hydrated. If you've been on your horse for more than ninety minutes, give him a break to eat. Riding a horse all day long is cruel, no matter what you weigh.

If you want to look better in the saddle, put a helmet on. Then work on your riding position. Let your body move with the horse, don't brace your legs, let your elbows breathe. Remember, horses have a stronger opinion about bad hands than any other body part.

Riding well is about transitions. Be gentle; ride rhythmic and smooth gait changes. Be soft in the seat of your saddle, go slow, and be polite.

Asking your horse to hold your weight at the halt, like gossiping cowboys with their legs hooked over their saddle-horns, is much harder for a horse than moving with weight on his back. When you're not riding, kindly get off his back.

Think about positive energy. Horses are good therapists, but leave your mental baggage at the mounting block. It's heavier for a horse to carry your depression and anxiety than a few extra pounds.

If you have no confidence, pretend you do. Fake it—breathe deep, ignore the outside noise, and know in your heart that you're right where you belong. Then let your horse carry you like family.

This is my secret game: Brag about your weight now and then, followed by a big fat smile. It's a stress-reliever for everyone. A woman who brags about her weight is someone who's unpredictable and probably crazy. Oddly, it cheers people up.

Most certainly be concerned about your health—your horse depends on you outliving him. Eat healthy food, do your own barn chores, and inhale horse manes regularly. Get a good athletic bra, a saddle that fits, and reward your horse, all the time, for the tiniest things. Then let the kindness you show your horse rub off on yourself as well.

Most of all, stop holding your breath. It makes you stiff and that anxiety is unattractive—*to your horse*. Pouch out your belly some, give your hips a wiggle and laugh out loud. Your horse will thank you. Maybe it's just your attitude that needs to lose some weight?

In case I'm not being obvious, these tips for overweight riders are also my tips for timid riders, or novice riders, or intermediate riders looking to improve their skills. Put your horse first. In the end, it's always about your horsemanship.

When people judge you, it says much more about them than it does you. Horses will judge you as well, but they don't care about your appearance, only that you actually *appear*, hopefully with a curry and a soft eye. You can trust horses; they will always judge the content of your character above the size of your breeches.

So set that weight free. It will never be the most important thing to your horse. Or people with any horse sense.

Horses and Tulips

At some distant moment in the past, probably after seeing *The Miracle of the White Stallions* when I was a kid, I found out that Spanish horses were started at four years old. Back then, I thought it was a terrible waste. Then a few years ago, I was at a nutritional seminar where the conversation turned to options to prepare long yearlings to start under saddle. And I thought the same thing—what a terrible waste. Then this week I read an article that said the optimal time to start a horse was seven years old, the age a horse has fully grown. So it goes, the horse world is not short on opinion.

I don't want to start a debate about who's right; what I notice is that horse lovers disagree from the start. We disagree on everything from age to training style to the right tack to use. Then we probably get defensive about it.

We compare the worst dressage rider to the best reiner, or the best eventer with the worst endurance rider, and judge each discipline by worst example. Let's not even start with breed preferences. Horse owners can't even agree on what constitutes abuse or neglect.

We run the full range of emotions starting with joy. Beyond that fear, despair, and sadness are probably inevitable along the way, and anxiety. Lots of anxiety. Then finally grief. We are long on passion for all kinds of horses. The crazy part is, we are debating with people who are on our side to begin with.

In the end, all of us are united: The most grizzled old rancher and the pinkest horse-crazy girl both get wet eyes and a runny nose remembering that certain horse.

The real problem isn't with each other. The real problem is that horses don't live long enough.

A horse's working life is an arc. There is the incline at the beginning; we are always in a hurry to get to the best start, whatever that is. Everything is training and aspiring. It's all looking ahead.

On the other end of the arc are the later years when arthritis is normal and the level of work starts to slide. He isn't as fast or strong, he gets reluctant to do what used to be easy, until the day that he can't hold us any longer. If you've done everything just right, he isn't any happier that day than you are.

There is a sweet spot between those extremes, when a horse is physically at his peak; he is mentally solid and capable, and his muscles are fully developed. He's working at his utmost and he's sound! It's an affirmation of all that he is... but that prime is finite, sandwiched between the years getting there, and the years reminiscing back.

We have to pick our battles: It's always a mistake with horses, you might win some fights with humans, but we never win against time. Even if the horse is thirty years old we always want one more season.

The real reason we get cranky is that horses are fragile. Horses seem bold and strong but we know their secret. That their feet are small and their digestive system is a bit unstable. Even if we are lucky and everything goes well, they just don't live long enough. Horses are heart-breakers. We know that in our hearts and we love them anyway.

This is the time of year that my friends in the northwest post photos of fields of tulips—so outlandishly beautiful with large petals in bold primary colors. And such frail flowers. I don't usually buy them cut because their petals bruise easily and their stalks go slack. Cut flowers are all about temporary beauty, and part of what we love about flowers is their transitory nature.

They just mark a small place in time, an occasion, with beauty. Cut or uncut, in a short time flowers wilt. And we shouldn't let their brevity ruin their loveliness or our appreciation of them.

Horses have so much more in common with tulips than oak trees, and that has to be part of what we love about them also. Even if it's the part we hate about loving them.

In our barn, we have two horses who've been retired as long or longer than they were ridden. We have one young horses working their plan for world domination, and a couple in undefined places and not happy about it. And we have one big shiny horse who is absolutely in his prime—confident and proud. It's just a snapshot. The best reason to have gratitude in this moment is that it can all change in a heartbeat.

It's tulip season again and that means most of our horses are another year older. Happy Birthday to the whole herd! It's easy to forget that every moment they are with us is a victory over so many obstacles. This year, let's celebrate the place we are in the journey right now—not the future and not the past—without blame toward ourselves or each other. Let's celebrate the elusive perfection and beauty of horses, and let's make peace with the rest.

How to listen to Your Horse

I had a friend who visited my farm during my first years here. She arrived for the weekend with books and wine. We'd cook and stay up late. In the mornings we took our coffee out into the pasture, still in our flannel pajamas, to look at wild-flowers.

I'm sure I talked about my horses too much, but she talked about everything else in the universe, so it was probably fair. She loved words and her voice had a musical quality. She never stopped talking and I didn't mind.

To say she wasn't a horse person was an understatement, but one visit she asked to ride.

Spirit was the best choice. Back in the day, before his promotion to Grandfather Horse, he was a tolerant guy who loved people who didn't know how to ride. Have you known horses like that? He found non-riders just a little less trouble. So I tacked him up, my friend mounted, and they went for a walk-about. I worked at barn chores but I could hear her chatting with him; the notes of her voice carried on the prairie breeze as they wandered through the pasture and around to the front of the property.

There were a few moments of silence, and then my friend squawked. I looked over and she was moving Spirit as fast as she could toward me, rocking in the saddle, kicking, and calling my name with one hand waving over her head as she urged him on. Eventually they got close, moving along at what you could only call a medium walk at best. Spirit will tell you there's a real up-side to non-riders.

"He talked to me! Spirit talked to me, I heard him." She was thrilled.

Usually I keep quiet about horse talk but after a couple of glasses of wine, I could've related a comment from my horse while telling a story, or maybe my friend was just surprised to hear another voice in her head.

"What did Spirit say?" She seemed excited but it wasn't like she was *really* riding him. I was sure she imagined it.

"Well, he told me to be quiet, that I talked too much, but still, I heard him," she said.

Dang, that was him all right. He didn't hold with chirpy drivel and one person's musical notes might be another horse's finger-nails on the chalk board.

"Yep. Sounds about right." Time for her to get down. She may have heard him, but now it was time to *listen*.

I love my friend, but let's be clear; if she can do it, so can you. Here is how to start: Clear the mental litter, like work rants and to-do lists from your mind. Leave real life at the barn door and let your brain settle and breathe. Now wait in the silence. This is the magic place.

If the first message you get is something like "*You need those thousand dollar breeches with the baby seal skin full-seat,*" or "*You really should fly to Spain and look for a pasture friend for me*", I'm guessing that it isn't actually your horse's voice you're hearing. Start over. Clear you mind of work drama again, lay down the baby seal club again, and keep your horse fantasies to yourself. Listen to the quiet, just be.

If you are grooming his rump and he nibbles at his flank, take your curry right there and go at it. Tell him *good boy*. It isn't a coincidence, he's pointing where it's itchy, so take him at his word. If he shows you another spot, go right there and reward him for asking again. Teach him to talk by listening.

All this gets more important once you hit the saddle and you hear his small voice say *My right shoulder is the stiff one.* What you actually notice is that he is counter-bent and now is when you normally pull that inside rein. Instead of your usual counter-attack, bring your calf quiet and sweet to that soft spot just at the girth and let him feel it quietly rest there, following each stride he takes. You don't have to kick him, just remind him that's where bend starts. No louder than that curry conversation while grooming, just consciously follow him.

He'll resist, reminding you that he isn't kidding, it's really stiff. You remember what a tight neck feels like, so your heel urges softness, like a warm touch. As your sit-bones ask for a forward, rhythmic walk, let your inside rein ask for a poll release for just an instant. Don't even hold it long enough for him to answer, it's just a suggestion that it might feel good to him to loosen his poll. Let him think before answering.

"As long as he stiffens his poll, he also stiffens all of his other limbs. We may therefore not try to address them until he has yielded in his poll." —E.F.Seidler, 1846

Your horse can't say it any clearer, his shoulder is tight, and you have a choice. Teach resistance by jerking the bit against the bone of his jaw, or you could release that inside rein just an inch and release his poll just enough to remind him what a release feels like. Just like he showed you the curry spot, show him a softness in your asking hand. Then a tiny ask again, opening your inside hand another inch, wider not back, and still in rhythm with his stride, while your inside leg supports his tight shoulder with warmth and softness. Think heating pad.

Give him a moment to read your intention to soften, and not fight. Keep walking and let him feel your patience with his shoulder. He will give it to you when he trusts your cue to release is not going to hurt and his muscles are warm. Releasing on cue, being supple, is how your horse tells you he trusts you to not bully him, but instead help him where it hurts. Just like the curry, this is a language you can build on. Trust = Relaxation.

It isn't any different than if someone grabbed your face. It's a decision you make to trust that person and surrender to a kiss, or flinch and escape. Asking for bend is just that intimate,

just that vulnerable. Violence is always a poor excuse for understanding—it's just common sense to distrust a bully.

Cowboys, Dressage Queens, and Respect

I got badmouthed by a cowboy recently. He dressed the part way too seriously.

It's okay, in dressage we think of ourselves as eternal students. There isn't a day that goes by that horses don't teach me something. I expect the same from people. I would have liked to have a friendly conversation with this cowboy, but he talked to my client behind my back, so I didn't get the chance.

Like every other riding discipline, there are some lowlife who wear the Western outfit, down to fringed chinks and neckerchief, but don't reflect the highest in the breed standard, if you know what I mean.

Sometimes the term cowboy has a bad connotation—to cowboy a horse around usually means rough handling. We've all seen enough shank-bit jerking, tie-down bracing, spur gouging, and general training profanity to last a life time.

But there are some dressage riders I wouldn't want to lay claim to either. Our breed standard runs the gamut as well. Intelligent horse people should never judge an entire group by the worst example. I'm reminding myself of that right now.

Dear Mr. Cowboy-outfit, a suggestion: when you see a woman with well-earned gray hair and an accent like mine, it's a safe bet that she probably didn't grow up in British riding yards where English saddles were the norm, or the Spanish Riding

School, learning elite equestrian principles while wearing full seat breeches and tall boots. More likely, I grew up like you; I rode whatever horse I could catch on the farm. I didn't have to choose between English and Western tack, because we had none of either. Yes, I'm suggesting we may be more similar than different.

I appreciate cowboys. Some of the kindest, most courteous people I know wear that *hat*. Mutual respect has always been part of that code toward both horses and other humans. And some percentage of cowboys have always trained horses using compassion and kindness, since cowboy-ing began.

Dear Mr. Cowboy-outfit, suggesting that the young horse I'm working with can be intimidated into training work faster is certainly one method. Or maybe if you watch a moment, you'll hear this horse tell you that violent approach has been tried already, and that's when his problem got bigger.

"The horse is a mirror. It goes deep into the body. When I see your horse I see you too. It shows me everything you are, everything about the horse. I try to face life for what it is. There's heartache, but it's a good thing. I'm trying to save the horse's life and your life too. The human is so good at war. He knows how to fight. But making peace, boy, that's the hardest thing for a human. But once you start giving, you won't believe how much you get back." —Ray Hunt

There was a time that I was happy in a Western saddle, slowly building from a lope to a gallop, leaving *11's* in my wake. If you haven't heard the term, *11's* refers to the marks on the ground left after a reining horse does a sliding stop. Yes, I'm a post-cowgirl who peeked through a door to a different kind of riding, one that intrigued me. The training process was slow but the results seemed ethereal. I decided to take up dressage with my reining horses.

Dear Mr. Cowboy-outfit, cowboys didn't actually invent horse training and not every horse will be improved by ranch work. And hard as it is to believe, there is a whole horse world out there, past the cows. It isn't that it's better or worse. It's that there is always more to learn and having an open mind is the best training aid that ever existed.

I knew a lifelong cowboy who was invited to a dressage barn to ride upper level horses for a month. He took the dare and when he returned, he sought me out for some gleeful dressage chat. His eyes were bright; he was filled with awe to have experienced a totally different dimension of horses. We chattered like dressage queens and his time riding dressage horses made him a better cowboy.

"It's amazing what you can learn after you've learned all that you think there is to learn." —Ray Hunt.

At the same time this week, I continued an ongoing conversation with a couple of other cowboys who are questioning the way they've always done things, wondering if there's a better way to work with horses, and asking my opinions. Conversations like this one can be so affirming on both sides. Every time people manage to evolve a bit, horses benefit.

Dear Mr. Cowboy-outfit, yes, I found a home in dressage, but I still share your heritage. America has a proud history of good horsemanship. We aren't gangsters, we are communicators. Suggesting that a horse will benefit from speed and fear demeans good trainers of any discipline.

"My belief in life is that we can all get along together if we try to understand one another... You'll meet a lot of people and have a lot of acquaintances, but as far as having friends—they are very rare and very precious. But every horse you ride can be your friend because you ask this of them. This is real important to me. You can ask the horse to do your thing, but you ask him; you offer it to him in a good way. You fix it up and let him find it. You do not make anything happen, no more than you can make a friendship begin." —Ray Hunt

Dear Mr. Cowboy-outfit, kindly don't assume that because I dress differently, I don't understand horses. Kindly don't assume, because I work quietly and slowly, that I am unskilled.

And because I still carry that cowboy heritage along in my dressage saddle, I wish you didn't reflect so badly on good horsemen and horsewomen who still wear the *hat*.

Left in the Dust: Your Ridiculously Slow Response Time

Have you noticed that horses are incredibly quicker than we are? I'm going to tell you the good news about that, but it's going to take a while to get there.

Horses have the fastest response time of any common domestic animal. Yes, they measure these things, and horses are quickest to perceive and respond to stimuli—partly because they are prey animals. Sharp awareness, coupled with the ability to flee immediately, is crucial to survive in the first place.

Conversely, humans have a conscious thought process that's arrogant enough that we think we know what's happening—without even using our senses. We think too much, to the point that we live in a dream state, a predator's luxury for sure. Although it's true that we do startle from time to time, we can also sleep through fires and earthquakes. Again, it's a miracle that natural selection gave us a wink and a nod.

I've heard the actual number: A horse's response time is seven times quicker than ours. We don't have a chance. How are we supposed to be the leader when we start this far behind?

Step one: Think less, sense more. Leave the thoughts of your day at the mounting block, along with any other benign intellectual activity. Instead of chattering away in your thoughts, get quiet and take in what your senses tell you. Start with your body; check for stiffness and when you find it, breathe into that tight area. Then feel your horse exhale and relax that area in his body. Is your horse's poll tight? Loosen your neck and jaw. Use a few moments to fluidly follow your horse's stride, like a mutual massage, connecting sit bones to spine. Then say thank you.

Horses live in the present moment, forever sensing their surroundings in real-time. They notice the environment in detail, but they don't wish it was summer. They are aware of every part of your body that's bigger than a fly, but they could care less about your Olympic aspirations. Horses are a bit Buddhist that way. So, bring your wandering, day-dreaming mind gently back and put it into your seat; settle into the inner world. If we want to have any chance of keeping up with our horses, we have to still our distracted thoughts and *feel the now.*

I know... *feel the now* is a bliss-ninny phrase that's boring and quiet, and it's so much easier to let your mind run like a rat-on-a-wheel, planning world domination, but stop. Go back and mentally get your horse. Change your point of view to his side.

The more rhythmically the horse moves, the more he relaxes, and to the degree that we take part in that, we become one with our horse. The only way to influence his brain is through his body, and he wants that conversation quiet and reciprocal.

When your brain is eventually quiet you can hear your horse speak. Does he have an opinion about your hands? Of course he does, and he's right. Listen to him. It doesn't mean that you can't ride on contact, it means that you need to let him teach you how to do it and he will do that by communicating through his body to yours, while you "listen" with each one of your senses. For all the physical drama of riding, it's a sport of interior awareness. Riding is the place where you and your horse's awareness align.

Any riding technique is only as good as the horse and rider's perception of each other.

You can strike a correct pose in the saddle, but your horse is looking for more communication than that, and he doesn't speak English. Follow him physically until you get to the vulnerable place inside where you can lead him mentally. Dressage riders are famous for riding with a seemingly blank stare in the vicinity of their horse's head. It's because they are not looking outside, so much as *feeling inside*. It's also called oneness.

Once we find that place of partnership, we can begin to negotiate asking the horse to come along, even if his response is faster than ours. Our guidance becomes a calming thing that provides him with a sense of well-being and with that confidence, he feels safe enough to respond in a less prey-extreme way. In other words, now your slow response time is something he likes about you. You begin to seem a bit presidential.

But then the two of you sense that fearful feeling of an almost imaginary thing, before the tiny thing, before the small thing, before the quiet thing, before the audible thing, before the accelerating thing, before the screaming bloody murder thing, and finally, the I-am-so-gone-dead-flop-sweat thing. Think eyes squinted shut, hands over ears, and an endless *la-la-la* screeching over top of everything. Your horse is responding badly and yes, seven times faster than you.

And at long last, here's the good news about your horse responding seven times faster: If you manage to stay present enough to maintain that physical communication that lets him feel you, and you give him a breath of help from your gut to his, even if it comes late, he will sense it immediately and remember that you're his safe place. And then he will come back to you seven times quicker as well.

I don't know if they can measure trust like they do reaction times, but if so, I'm guessing that increases about seven times, too.

How to Teach Your Horse to Hate Arena Work

Does your horse go better out of the arena? It seems like some horses just won't go forward and no amount of kicking and yelling by the rider works. Sometimes they're gate sour: fast toward the gate but then getting away from the gate is a wrestling match. Horses who are normally quiet and good become cranky and drag their toes in the arena, counter-bent and tense.

Riders tell me that their horse is bored in the arena. I notice that there is a predictable coincidence between how a rider feels about things and how her horse responds.

It goes like this: we head into the arena. Let's say he's sound and responsive most of the time. There's no problem when he's ridden in the pasture. Now in an arena, things change. Even if there's no traffic, the rail beckons a rider and for the first time, there is a place his feet need to be, so maybe we use our reins more than in the pasture. There are actual corners to navigate and he's nowhere near where he should be, so even more steering is in order. We correct each stride, trying to get him to a particular place, not noticing it's already too late for him to make it.

Maybe there are dressage letters posted. Even western barns have them because it's easier for a trainer to say *circle at B* than *circle at the fifth post*. So we decide to circle at B, but start too late and then act like there's a cliff just past B that might kill all of us. One more hard pull with the inside rein. He pulls back, of course, and tosses his head. Then we correct him even louder because the position of the silly letter means he's wrong.

In the arena most riders feel watched, even if no one is there. So we get self-conscious. If there are other riders, or worse yet, a trainer, it means every stride is visible to the world. Of course they must be judging us…so we decide to out-judge them, as if skill is defined by being our own worst critic.

Then we drill it and drill it—closer to the rail, more bend, deeper in the corner, bigger stride, and more cross over at the leg yield. If we have a few good tries, we celebrate by doing more, just in case the crowd didn't see the first few. Then the horse begins to dull, of course. He thinks he's doing what he's being asked for, but the cue continues again and again. There's no release or reward, so he loses confidence and tries something else. While trying to find the right thing, he stops doing the right thing. Then we push harder, just one more and we can quit, but he has given you a stack of good tries already and now he's as frustrated as we are. Nag-nag-nag. What horse wants to be in the arena with you? Did no one ever teach you to say thank you?

The horse's opinion of arena work is much simpler. "Everything I do is wrong." And that sounds just like I *hate* the arena.

To add insult to injury, there is some idiot on a horse, smiling and laughing while her horse is doing beautiful, complicated work. She isn't even trying and her horse *likes* the arena. Gotta hate that, when you are so serious and some giggle-puss, undeserving rider gets lucky. Add a bit of envy to the mix.

Sometimes riding in the arena gets too precious. And it's my job to remind you that every time you're in the saddle, you're training your horse. So yes, congrats on training your horse to hate the arena.

But the good news is that every time you're in the saddle, you're training your horse! This is easy to fix.

If your horse is better out of the arena, that might be an answer. Ride *AS IF* you're out. I'm not sure trail riding is more fun for a horse than the arena; I do know riders don't constantly correct their horse's every move on the trail. Ride in the arena as if it's a huge meadow and there's no wrong place to be. Let him move big—take up all the space you need. Go on a long rein and give him time to warm his joints. Then pat him and give him even more time.

Less correction, more direction.

Ride like nobody's watching and if you aren't prepared for the circle by B, then do it past B. Don't punish him because you didn't prepare in time. Have a plan for what you want to work on, but don't care about it too much. In other words, set him up to succeed. Relaxed and forward gaits are always a bigger priority than anything else, because they are required before a horse can actually do anything else.

Change things up. In dressage, we believe doing transitions is how we get a horse's attention. The small print says that doesn't mean the same transition again and again. Step one is to ride freely, to encourage a supple and fluid body. Dressage rhymes with massage for a reason. Past that, it's the rider's job to get creative. When you canter, ride for the horizon. When you walk, breathe slowly like you're passing a pond. If you get stuck in a corner without a plan, use the default plan—laugh and start over. Partners don't blame each other.

And in this perfect moment, whether it's a mountain meadow with wild flowers or inside a dark, dusty indoor arena, remember you are in a sacred, sweet place—being lifted and carried by a horse. Today is irreplaceable. Thank him every chance you get.

Respecting Your "Other" Space

I assume your horse respects your space; that on the ground he stands a couple of feet away, relaxed and cool. He doesn't shove his shoulder into you, or jerk the lead rope out of your hands, or perform impatient body searches looking for hidden surprises.

Please tell me I'm right. Because it reflects your consistency with small corrections, as well as his general level of confidence. Consistency is the best kindness we can show a horse. When he knows what's expected and gets rewarded, there are fewer mood swings, less anxiety, and a more positive overall ride. For both of you.

Horse behavior runs in tendencies. If every time you transition to a walk, he falls on his forehand and sashays along, dragging his toes, then every transition back to the trot will have fight and drag—you'll need to over-cue him and he'll get tense. A tendency of resistance is born.

Better to give him a release from work with the reins, but continue the good forward rhythm at the walk, building a consistent positive tendency of balance and energy. The willingness to go forward is one of the biggest issues we nag about and if we have just inadvertently asked him to dawdle, it's our fault. Our brain (seat) quit riding and he took the cue.

As he loses forward it impacts his balance so he might counter bend or even think about grazing. It happens in a heartbeat; he pulls his head and then we wake up and pull it back. It feels like he has a head issue when the real problem was the instant before that when his rhythm broke. The correction for losing forward is more leg but we've pulled the reins. Now the horse is more resistant yet and we cued the whole face fight from the beginning.

And the truth: Horses like small cues and we humans instinctively over-use our hands. When he slowed down, instead of cuing his body, we corrected his face. We're not even on the same page—it's as if you asked for a drink and were given a book.

What if the truth is that he isn't disobedient, but instead he's taking every cue, even the ones we aren't even aware we're giving? A horse's response time is seven times faster than ours. It's totally possible.

Assuming you're a normal human, who naturally thinks with her hands instead of her seat, now he's stuck on your tight rein and you're kicking hard enough to bruise your horse's ribs, so he's bracing his flank. He thinks you cued that too. It's still a partnership, but now the tendency is running backward.

Throw down your reins and let him walk. Any speed, just walk. Feel your sit-bones flow with his back. Remember how good that feels? And your legs follow the swing of his barrel back and forth.

Rhythm that is broken by the reins is restored with the seat.

While that relaxed forward walk is simmering along, think about the other space that your horse isn't respecting—the space between your knees.

Back when he first lost forward, in the split second just before his head moved, his shoulders changed. Maybe one collapsed or shifted to the outside, but either way, it was a leg correction that was needed. Now do a couple of transitions and when you feel him fall off the rail or make an unplanned turn, feel his movement through your knees and legs. Ignore his head, be *disarmed*. Just feel him with your body. Teach yourself to recognize when leg is needed. Notice how much your hands want to take the bait and begin to re-train yourself to rest your hands.

If you are moving straight and he throws a shoulder through your leg, the correction needed is made with the displaced leg. Ask him to stand tall again. Putting awareness in that cuing leg might be enough. But just like ground work, you might have to bump him to respect your space...the space between your knees.

As you prepare to turn, maybe he's stiff and you feel the universal urge to pull the inside rein. Let that nasty rein urge be a cue to *YOU* to use more leg. Again, feel him between your knees. Think of your legs as a tunnel your horse is going through: if it's a straight tunnel, he moves straight, respecting your legs. If it's a curve, then turn your waist and feel your inside knee open as your outside knee closes. Trust him to curve. Let your hands and shoulders follow your waist turn in unity, but keep focus on cuing with your seat and legs.

If your waist is turning, your body is supple and that's the cue you want to give—to be supple. If there is a second he resists that, our first instinct is to ask harder with our hands. I repeat, this instinct to use our hands is almost irresistible, but leave your hands still. If he needs more energy from you to take the cue, give it with your legs and seat. It's the very definition of counter-intuitive, but if you can feel him resist that outside knee, that same knee is the aid you answer with. Ask him to stay between your legs by correcting his shoulder with your leg, not a louder rein. Leave his face out of it for now. Too often, when our brain reacts, our hands escalate the conversation too quickly: a bit is always metal on bone.

In dressage, we ride an invisible interior line from your inside foot to your outside rein. It's a supple, fluid cue that's given body to body. It creates a connection that is literally more than skin deep; oneness is the reward. Don't let your hands cheapen it.

Ride consistently aware in the saddle; feel his conversation with you and respect him enough to ask for his best answer. It's the true definition of positive training.

When Horses Go Through Menopause

Disclaimer: I'm not a vet. Or a doctor. But someone has to talk about it.

How can you tell your horse is going through menopause? Here are some of the symptoms: His rider is usually a woman somewhere in her forties or older. Well, I guess there is just that one symptom really.

Still, when horses go through menopause, it's a frightening experience. As hormone levels start bouncing up and down, symptoms can be overwhelming. Although the horse doesn't experience the same night sweats, hot flashes, urinary issues, joint pain, skin dryness, and bone loss as his rider might, he does share the same emotional symptoms.

Common emotional symptoms of (peri)menopause are depression, anxiety, mood swings, reduced self-esteem, rage, irritability, crying easily and feeling overwhelmed. I confess, there have been times in my life that this would be considered a normal day at the barn. Keep riding.

And while I am getting the bad news out of the way, there's this: *Perimenopause symptoms typically continue throughout a woman's monthly cycle and do not disappear once she gets her period. They are also much more erratic, unpredictable and intense. So much so that many women feel they are losing control or as if they are going crazy.* (from Perimenopause and the

Emotional Rollercoaster by Mia Lundin) Meaning menopause is like PMS but it doesn't go away for a few years. Keep riding.

Is Equine Menopause real? Yes. Does your horse suffer from these symptoms? Yes, he catches them from you.

I will leave the medical part to people who know more. The part that concerns me is this: At this point in our riding lives–because of hormonal changes–some of us lose confidence. It's tied into emotions, fueled by hormonal changes that are real, not hypochondria. We don't need to punish ourselves, any more than a migraine sufferer punishes themselves for getting a migraine. I remind you—lots of people had a fear of horses their whole lives. You did not. Keep riding.

The part that really drives me crazy, or should I say, menopausal, is that our culture tells us that feelings of anxiety—like vulnerability, fear, or even being timid are signs of weakness, which makes it the fault of the victim. Let's be clear: It isn't our fault and we are not victims.

Some of us stop riding–we break our own hearts with a quiet dismount. Some of us get a young, hot horse and act like balding middle-aged men in Corvettes. We each have our own path.

We may be *old gray mares* to some, but years have given us wisdom and that's a good trade, especially where horses are concerned.

For some of us of a certain age, our taste in partners has changed. At one point in our lives we might have loved a whiskey-drinking, bank-robbing bad boy on a motorcycle and then at another point in life, the charms of a computer programmer cannot be over-stated. Don't be embarrassed, brag about it!

It's true with horses too. Maybe now is the time for a mid-life gelding who doesn't want to jump anymore. No shame, keep riding.

How to deal with the emotional concerns that are part of menopause? Health professionals recommend exercise and eating healthy. That's what they recommend for most everything. Along with seeking emotional support from friends and family; I think horses fall into that category.

And also they encourage having a creative outlet or hobby that fosters a sense of achievement. This is the part that is tricky in the barn. Horses are a fantastic creative outlet and way more rewarding to most of us than crochet will ever be, but achievement is a subjective thing.

Maybe it's time to be as kind to yourself as you are to your horse—who I remind you, goes through menopause with you. If you are not young enough to ride stupid anymore, that's good news. Ride smarter, not stronger. Work on relationship—it has always been women's strong suit. Use your age-given wisdom to negotiate a peaceful path with subtle cues. Leave the pulling and jerking to hormone-driven youth. Buy yourself a purple saddle pad and use the mounting block. But know the truth; in some ways, you are capable of riding better now than ever before. Especially in your horse's opinion.

Wisdom comes with a better understanding of patience, the most important skill a rider can have. Young skin, white breeches, and all the elite training in the world will never take the place of patience to a horse. A post-menopausal *old gray mare* in the saddle is a gift to a horse. And what do you have to lose at this age? The barn door is flung open to ride your own ride.

And a last bit of advice from a trainer: For crying out loud, stop apologizing for not wanting to get bucked off. I hear this all the time from clients, as if the best riders pray for unplanned air-time. Not wanting to get bucked off might be the most rational thing you have said since you bought your first horse. Brag about it—what's the point of surviving everything before menopause, if we're going to get stupid now? Wear a helmet, but *keep riding.*

When to Dismount and
Say Thank You

"Asking your horse to hold your weight at the halt, like gossiping cowboys with their legs hooked over their saddle-horns, is much harder for a horse than moving with weight on his back. When you're not riding, kindly get off his back."

This quote is from last week's blog and Cathy asked me to elaborate. I promised I'd hold it to a moderate rant.

Let's start by having a good ride. That means a warm-up that is patient and pleasant. The horse has longer reins and is striding up with a nice rhythm. His poll is soft and the rider is breathing deeply. You turn your waist and ask him to reverse and in that movement, you feel his ribs stretch to the outside while his inside ribs soften around your leg. Dressage rhymes with massage for a reason. Repeat a few times, asking for longer steps with your seat, and then shorter. Sweet. Good boy.

Relaxed and forward, just like the training pyramid says. Now some walk-trot transitions, still a long rein and you can feel him lift and carry you. The strides are slow enough to be big, and from the tip of his nose to his tail, there's a swinging rhythm that flows under you like a river. He's using himself well, and his back is starting to lift.

What happens next depends on riding discipline and the level of horse/rider proficiency, but *whatever* happens next is aided by the fifteen to twenty minutes you just spent helping your horse slowly warm his muscles. He feels good in his body and he is ready to work. Reining, dressage, jumping; he's warm and willing. So let's say you do a light bit of training and when he tries, he gets a scratch.

"Ask often, be content with little, and reward greatly." It's always smart to channel Nuno Oliveira.

The horse is happy, the rider is happy, and after fifteen or twenty minutes of training, there is a long cool down that feels just as good at the end of the ride as the beginning. Moving forward, swinging big lets him step under with his hind leg and he gets stronger with every stride. So the rider asks for a halt and gives her horse a pat. Then maybe there is another lesson to watch, or a friend to chat with. Now might be a good time to check messages on your smartphone. Is there anything better than sitting on a horse?

Except that you just had a generous, fluid ride, asking him go light and forward, and now you're parked in the saddle being dead weight pushing down on his spine, which he has just politely lifted for you. Kind of squishing all that happy, round work. It's not great for a young horse, but for a mid-life or older horse who has the beginnings of arthritis, the benefits of the ride get minimized, just when they're needed even more.

A brief physics lesson: Carrying a stack of books while walking forward is an example of dynamic force. Similarly, a forward horse spends less effort carrying weight because of that dynamic movement. Standing still and holding a stack of books is a static load, the force is downward. Can you feel it, maybe in your back? So we shift weight from one foot to the other because it's harder to hold static weight and maintain balance. Make any sense?

That's when you hear her, "Drives me nuts!" It's Kim Walnes- she's in your arena! "Your horse is not a sofa!" Okay, she isn't in your arena, but it would be nice. She did write this on the blog last week, just after Cathy asked for clarification.

Physics is reason enough, but there is an even more

important reason to get off, and as usual, it's about your horse's state of mind. Riders underestimate the importance of the last thing they do before dismounting.

Horses learn in hindsight. They always remember the thing-before-the-thing. They are smart that way; survival often depends on it. So if bad things happen every time he gets caught, or if riding in the trailer bothers his stomach, or if what happens after the mounting block feels like punishment, he is bright enough to do the math and the thing before, whatever that is, becomes a cue to resist.

But with beauty and grace, the reverse is also true. If we give a horse a happy release just as he has done good work, he remembers that just as well. Release is the best reward; it's honest, loud, and true. Giving him a long rein and a scratch makes him remember the previous thing. Parking on his back like a cinder block after good work deflates the value of the training moment, but vaulting off, loosening the girth, and letting him be done will tattoo that moment in his mind like a big red heart with your name across it on a blue ribbon. Think of dismounting as an effective training aid.

Sometimes in competitions, you'll see a wonderful rider finish, jump down, and walk their horse out. I always think that's what makes them a great rider; the ability to say thank you in another language.

Quitting on a high note leaves your partner positive and wanting more. Let that be enough. Don't linger—get off and say thank you. Then maybe next time he'll volunteer to noodle with you at the mounting block.

Helmets, Gravity, and
Human Superiority

August 1 is International Helmet Awareness Day. It's the day that the organization Riders4Helmets was founded, in the wake of U.S. Olympian Courtney King-Dye's traumatic brain injury, to raise awareness and promote equestrian helmet use. Helmet retailers join in by giving discounts.

This is the fifth year and every year I write about helmets because it's so important. Every year, I repeat statistics like this: Equestrians are twenty times more likely to sustain an injury than a motorcycle rider, or that speed makes no difference. A surprisingly high number of brain injuries happen while mounting. Last year I wrote about nearly getting in a bar fight on the topic. Previously, I wrote about a woman younger than I am, in a nursing home, who haunts me still; she's living my biggest personal fear. Every year riders who wear helmets cheer this day. Preaching to the choir is easy–and the other side is dug in and defensive.

If helmet use was about needing logical proof, overwhelming statistics about brain injury would convince people. There is no debate. Helmets are like seat belts; they save lives. Still, we had to pass a law. We pride ourselves in being the superior species but still put our politics above our intellect and common sense. Everyone has heard it all before and it's disheartening. Even now, mothers ride without helmets, mothers allow their children to ride without helmets. There's an argument that this conversation is hopeless. Does stubborn, self-defeating, belligerent foolishness—masquerading as personal choice—ever wear you down?

Instead of more ranting, can I tell you what I love about gravity? It's dependable, as consistent and fair as any notion around. Gravity has no respect for governments or religions. No respect for emotions or personal codes. Gravity is a natural law. It's never up for re-election, it isn't racist or sexist or ageist or any other 'ist' imaginable. Gravity treats each of us equally regardless of income. Amen to that.

It's enough to give you a real love of black and white distinctions in our world of gray excuses. There's no buy-out. It isn't personal. No one gets a pass, and as much as humans love to think they are the exception to the rule, none of us are. Preach personal choice all you want. Defy gravity on moral or ethical grounds. Have at it.

But gravity will ignore us and our arrogance, while it pulls us down to collide with the truth.

What is it about humans that we squander our gifts? How did we get so ungrateful as to value our brain so little? I understand and respect ignorance, but how did it come to pass that willful stupidity became a valid choice? We lose horse-crazy little girls and strong equine professionals and backyard riders all the time. We languish in hindsight, wishing we had a do-over and even with that knowledge, some of us still think we are immune. None of us is that lucky.

In the end, gravity will win. Before that, Alzheimer's will take some of us. It's as uncontrollable as gravity. None of us knows the future, but of all the gifts I'm blessed with, it's my mind that I value the most; it's my door to a world of wonder and beauty and freedom.

Last year someone posted a comment on my blog that I saved in my file of statistics. A woman said, "I wear one especially when on green horses because my daughter-in-law refuses to change my diapers."

I had to laugh. My good brain will always giggle at gallows humor. It's funny, unless of course you remember a young woman, confined in a nursing home, wearing diapers. Humans. We're supposed to be the smart ones but we could take a lesson in self-preservation from all the other "less-evolved" species.

How to Ride Like a Kid

Remember riding when you were a kid? We climbed on top from a gate or a truck bumper. No bridle, no saddle, no worries. Remember the way the sun felt on our shoulders? If it was hot enough, there was a thin layer of sweat between our horse and our cut-offs—intermingled sweat. We didn't take lessons, we were free. In our mind's eye, when we look down we see our tan legs against his flank and sometimes our colors ran together. We were chestnut tan from the sun; we were dirty bay at the end of the day. It was fun and wild and we didn't always make it back for lunch. We were fearless.

May I break in on this idyllic memory for a moment? There are a few reasons it went so well; first off, we didn't fight. Most of us had no steering and didn't care; if our horse didn't go where we wanted, we went where he wanted. The plan was to ride; that was good enough. If we were still on an hour or two later—it was a great ride. If we had to get off and lead our horses, that was good, too. It was summer. We had low expectations and no thought of controlling anything.

As adults, we get to the mounting block carrying a mental load that weighs four times what we do. And those are just the day-to-day stresses: time, money, relationships. We bring a list of things to do, but we don't exactly remember what's on the list. Still we hold on. Most of all, we are on a time schedule. Maybe there is a show coming, or we have another appointment, but usually it's because we're in a hurry all the time and it's a habit now. All of this, and we aren't in the saddle yet.

The biggest killer of the long-lost kid-ride? We worry about how we ride, how we look, how our horse looks; even if we don't compete, we judge it all—usually harsher than a trainer or judge would. We have self-doubt. Sometimes it's just a feeling; a sticky green nonspecific frustration with a red rickrack fringe of impatience. It doesn't look good on anyone.

In truth, I don't know if our childhood rides were actually all that blissful. I doubt it. I do know that we're more self-conscious now, and it gets in our way. Maybe if we heard our thoughts in someone else's voice they'd sound silly, but inside our heads, they seem sacred and true, and a bit more so each time we repeat them. Our favorite jab—we wish we rode like we did as kids. Even if we didn't actually ride as kids, we still have that fantasy.

So, we grew up and got self-conscious—feeling an over-sized awareness that included uncomfortable emotions like embarrassment and nervousness. Self-consciousness comes with judgment. Humility is good, but if our confidence suffers, so does our leadership. Then we sit on our horse's back talking to ourselves about our horse and his problems. We leave him out of the conversation entirely. Meanwhile our horse is out there in the real world looking for some help.

We can't become children again. Our hormones see to that. And frankly, riding like we did when we were kids was dangerous and if we keep doing that indefinitely, our guardian angels will give up on us.

Maybe the closest we could get to being childlike again is to replace self-conscious thought with self-aware thought. Less judgment and more openness. It means experiencing the world through our senses instead of our intellect. It's closer to how kids and horses do it.

Here is where your riding instructor sounds like a yoga teacher. The first step is the hardest: to let our brain rest and open our senses to listen and feel. Breathe. Then be aware of your breath. Count an inhale, one-two-three. Feel your body soften. Exhale, one-two-three. Feel his strides under you lifting your sit-bones one at a time.

"Is he forward enough? Why is he fighting my contact?"

Yes, that's the voice of the self-conscious judging part of your brain. This is important: be kind to it. If you judge yourself harshly for having a thought; if you feel like you need a whip and spurs to push those thoughts out of your mind, then start over. Be gentle with yourself, excuse those thoughts with a breeze of a breath. When they come back again in a few seconds—no problem. Breathe them away again and replace those thoughts with the feel of his barrel relaxing. One-two-three, soften your jaw. Feel your horse follow suit.

(Yes, I am aware that this is my two millionth essay on breathing, cleverly disguised. But I mean it, there is nothing more important.)

Every time you breeze-away a thought, know that you're being lifted and held in a sacred place. Be grateful and feel your heart melt. You can keep your adult insecurities; be critical and doubting *out* of the saddle if you need to, but for these few mounted moments, let go. Let your ribs expand, soften your belly, be aware but thought-less.

It's about then, in a connected moment, that you feel his stiff shoulder or his tense poll. All horses have tension, but this time you feel it small and without judgment. You let your leg massage his ribs back and forth, while you count your breath, one-two-three, and give him time. He isn't pretending and this is an opportunity to hear him with physical kindness. The same kindness that you've shown yourself.

And with a breath, you excuse this good thought as well; one-two-three, and in this discipline of breath and mind, there is freedom from reaction and judgment.

There you are, riding like a kid. Easy as one-two-three.

Behavior, Personality, and Anxiety

Can you tell the difference between personality, who a horse is, and behavior, what a horse does?

With people it can be a bit easier because we are used to separating the two. We're taught to "hate the sin and love the sinner." Most of us know someone who is kind and funny, but a hot mess when they're drunk. This is progress from generalized beliefs about groups resulting in racism, sexism and all the other "isms"; better than grouping people together without concern for who they are as individuals.

Horses are honest animals. It's a rare and crazy thing that a prey animal should volunteer to partner with a predator, but they do. When watching foals play, they are curious, tentative, smart, and agile. They are born ready to respond to reward and they are easily frightened. We have a vote in what happens next.

I know a horsewoman who prides herself on being good with horses. She owns a small herd and tells me, over time, that each one of the horses is hot. It's just who they are. There are young horses, old horses, and several breeds, but each of them has behavioral problems that look nearly identical. Did I mention her hands are brutal?

When they don't listen at the walk, she sends them to the trot, and when that comes apart, she pushes them to the canter. She just rides them through it. She runs them fast and hard to get the energy out of them and she is a brave rider. Eventually they become exhausted and give in. Lots of us were trained to do it this way and it even works to a small degree for some horses. But for others, their anxiety accelerates to hysteria and becomes a chronic pattern. It's how an elder horse can still be dangerous. And I'll say, misunderstood. Is he really hot or honestly fearful of the pain and tension felt from his rider?

Historically women were judged too high-strung and emotional for many jobs. We were excused from important positions because we were inadequate by virtue of our sex. We might as well have been name-called Arabians, for all the false assumptions that were made.

In the end, horses are some combination of DNA, accident of birth, and experience. We can't change the past for them, but we can improve their experience. We can reshape their future.

This is where recognizing anxiety becomes important. When you see a horse with wild eyes, a stiff neck, and a tense tap-dance of hooves, it's easy to recognize the short list of negative behaviors. Is he mad or aggressive? Is he hot and crazy? Does he need to be exhausted for his brain to kick in? Or does he have some sort of plan to personally humiliate you, or ruin your breeches because they're expensive, or test you for some random reason that he made up when you didn't give him a carrot when you haltered him. And who is it sounding unbalanced now?

The foundation of dressage says that a horse should be relaxed. We don't do it to please the judge, we do it for the good of the horse. It should be obvious to a rider that a horse can't learn if he's afraid. Or more truthfully, can't learn anything positive. He can learn humans are callous and cruel leaders. We can train him to know we have no compassion.

There is one other option. Instead of running him into the ground or psychoanalyzing him, how about helping him relax? Instead of pushing him to distrust you at even faster gaits, how about walking and giving him enough rein to breathe. It isn't as dramatic. It takes more skill and patience than bravado. And you have to listen to the inside of your horse instead of being distracted by exterior behavior. First you have to remember who he is and then you have to remind him. It's what a positive leader does.

Because even if you can ride through the behavior, anxiety is a killer. Anxiety is the base ingredient in your horse's overall well-being and has a direct connection to his health, happiness, and long-term soundness and ride-ability.

Here is the physical part: a horse's adrenal glands are located in front of the kidneys in the lower back. It's their job to manage stress by producing the anti-inflammatory hormone cortisol, as well as the hormone adrenaline, when the fight-or-flight response is activated.

If anxiety and stress become a habit, the adrenal glands become over-worked, causing adrenal fatigue or burnout. Horses struggling with adrenal fatigue show symptoms that can seem a bit bi-polar; they are excitable but with little stamina, meaning short bursts of energy in between crashes. They can be unpredictable, often having complete meltdowns over seemingly little things.

Chronically anxious horses have a high rate of stomach ulcers and colic. It's also proven that stress affects the immune system, so these horses have a harder time fighting off illness, and are more likely to suffer more severe reactions to insect bites, parasites, and vaccinations.

Do you still want to screw up your courage and dominate him through his fit? Statistics also tell us that a huge number of rescue horses are given up because of behavioral problems. How many of those horses could be good partners if we had dealt with the real problem instead of fighting the symptoms in the first place? When will we finally learn to listen and not take his clear message as an insult to our egos? And even if you don't want to do better for your horse, how is this level of stress working for you?

Breathe. *Give peace a chance.* Sing it at the walk.

Consistency:
Doing Math in the Saddle

Consistency is a great aid but do you know how it actually works? There's an analogy I heard decades ago that has stuck with me. It involves bank accounts. You're right; never listen to me about money, but it's not that kind of bank account.

Start by thinking that you and your horse each have a bank account of experience. For your horse it's a reckoning of all of his experiences with humans—all the good times and all those times where he got scared and had no help. Confidence, fear, willingness to partner, and what caused pain and when rewards were given. The account is his possession. He's the one who quantifies the contents.

Your account has all of your horsemanship experiences, including the times you were confident or fearful. It's what you have learned from experts and how well you listen to your horse. You get extra points for patience. A tiny corner is reserved for your dreams. It's your personal wealth as a potential partner for a horse.

It's simple—in any situation, either of you can make deposits or withdrawals. An experienced rider can help a young horse with a deposit of patience and positive training. An old campaigner can enrich a novice rider by carrying them through a rough spot. Sometimes it's referred to as the Twenty Year Rule; for the best results the sum of experience shared by the horse and rider should equal twenty years or so.

It makes perfect sense; all of us are the sum of our experience. But there was one problem. Back then, I had a very green and spooky young horse and I wasn't as brave and crazy as when I was a kid. Bankrupt. Neither of us had much to draw on. We had good intentions but it was an against-the-odds start.

It's a pretty common dilemma. Most rideable horses that end up in rescue have training problems, stemming from poor handling. Some riders manage to buy a well-trained horse, but without the right skills, the horse's account is quickly depleted and he becomes resistant and sour. A rider's good intentions can become spent on a confused horse, as well.

Seen this way, it's a fair, impartial accounting of any situation, whether it's a competition horse or a trail horse. Seeing a horse/rider problem as a math equation takes some of the emotion and blame out of it on both sides and that's a great first step. Guilt and failure are negative deposits.

Start now. The past is data; you can't change that, so let it be. Horses have strong memories and if that trait is working against you, your best hope is to layer good memories on top that will eventually out-number the bad. You have to get the numbers in his favor. If your confidence is shaky, or you need a few more training tools, then make that investment in getting good, professional help and watch your own numbers go up.

Here is where consistency comes in. Horses love a routine and it's the sacred job of every rider to leave the horse in a better place at the end of the ride than the beginning. It's our version of *First Do No Harm.*

Just like the stock market, horses are always moving in an overall tendency. They are getting better or worse. Long-range investments have less drama and are more dependable, while others think taking their life savings to Vegas for the weekend is a smart bet. It's a choice.

Start your ride start slowly with a warm-up that relaxes and supples him. Reward him for being alive. Get happy. Notice him liking what you're saying; reward that. On this one day, the most you can do is have one ride. Lower your expectations of perfecting your world in an instant. Instead of getting greedy, be content to make one good deposit.

The truest thing that I know about horses is that it's time and consistency that trains a horse. There are no shortcuts, no get-rich-quick schemes, that will ever take the place of a simple Piggy Bank approach.

The thing we pay attention to grows. If we make a problem bigger than it is by isolating it and scrutinizing it into a huge issue, then we squander an opportunity. We can invest worry until the issue blocks out the daylight or invest in knowing it all works out in hindsight. Because it really does.

Here's the secret: never give up. Get a tortoise tattoo if you need to, but just stick it out, slowly and patiently, because consistency is the greatest kindness a horse will ever know. He wants the confidence to clearly understand where he should be, without fear of pain. One positive ride at a time, consistency will buy you a new normal.

You know that rider you see who is smiling, riding a dream horse that will do anything? That horse people call a push-button horse? They focused on what was right about their ride and built their fortune one penny at a time. It was no accident; it was a long-term goal. Praise their consistency.

And then one day, if you are very, very lucky, you will take a short twenty-minute ride on a green and frightened horse. In those moments you will have a wealth of understanding and positive leadership to give him. You will be an aid to him. Then he will exhale that first shallow blow of baby trust, as you exhale a breath rich in the memory of that first horse you invested your best self in. Be rich in the knowledge that you have something of value to offer a horse.

It's about Greeks and Romans,
Even Today

Is there a natural way to ride a horse? Is it possible to ride in such a way that the horse goes willingly forward, without constriction, as if he were moving at liberty? Is there a path to a different sort of ride, where kindness and understanding are the primary aids? Or should work look like struggle?

Spit has been flying on the internet this week. There's dressage news from the FEI European Championships at Achen and I have to defend my chosen riding discipline one more time. Flash: there was rollkur—hyper-flexion of the neck—done by dressage riders there. Yes, it's against the rules; but more than that, it insults the beauty and integrity of our historical tradition. And yet even more than that, it physically disables horses.

I should add that there is a public facility down the road from my barn, filled with riders in western saddles, shank bits and vicious spurs, jerking away mindlessly on their horse's bits, metal on bone, doing as bad or worse—instructors and students alike. Despicable. Not the disciplines; it isn't about tack or what we ask the horse to do under-saddle. It's about *how* we ask.

Disclaimer: I harp on this topic all the time but it's been a sad week. A brilliant and talented dressage stallion was retired too young, with a lameness related to forceful rollkur training. Locally, a horrendous, long-winded abuse trial, involving a starved herd with over half dead on the ground, ended with a marginal sentence that's being appealed. When I first came to dressage, the best horses were just coming into their prime in their teens. Now young horses are being started earlier and earlier, long before they have finished growing and built the strength required to even carry a rider, much less compete. The line between a kind, responsive partner and a broken-down rescue horse is defined by a rider's awareness and sensitivity all too often—and at every level of riding. So I'm mad, too.

Want a history lesson? Some of the first writing we have about horses is from ancient Greece. Simon and Xenophon wrote about the art of riding:

"For what the horse does under compulsion... is done without understanding; and there is no beauty in it either, any more than if one should whip and spur a dancer." —Xenophon, b. 430BC

At that time, Euripides was writing plays and the Parthenon was just finished. The Greeks loved culture: art, music, dance. And riding horses.

At the same time, other cultures like the Romans were more barbaric, more materialistic, and less enlightened. It isn't a value judgment so much as a statement of priorities. Horses were treated more harshly in those cultures where warriors used them as tools. Romans left no writing about horses during these years.

Through the centuries, these two approaches to riding continued. The equestrian art was increased by one culture, but then "bastardized by war" in another. And so on to today. Sometimes we are evolving with sensitivity as riders, and sometimes we're using brutality as a means to an end.

"Under no circumstance should your hand disturb the horse's mouth. You must learn to stay calm in all situations and control your emotions. There is no room for anger." —Xenophon

There is no trainer in this world who raises their hand and proudly says, "I train with violence and cruelty." Yet dressage riders are excused from the arena when there are traces of blood on their horse's bit. Men in cowboy hats make videos of themselves whacking horses in the head with whips–while holding a lead rope tight and playing to the crowd—and pass it off as horsemanship.

Everyone has a good line. Everyone defends their technique in positive terms but walking the talk is a different thing. We actually have to demonstrate that our actions match our words. We don't like what we see, so to many of us competition is the same thing as abuse. Riders who train with finesse and kindness do compete and win. We need to peacefully claim back that ground, especially in the show arena. It's a challenge to maintain focus in a storm of show reality and easy to fail our ideals. And brutality will always come easier to a predator, a human being, than vulnerability and honesty. We need to stand up for horses; to step out past our comfort zone and let our voice for kind training be heard, and more so, seen in our happy, relaxed horses.

Nuno Oliveira defines dressage as a conversation with a horse on a higher level, one of courtesy and finesse. Times change but classical principles remain: the horse should be a partner and not a slave. The goal of equestrian art is the perfect understanding with our horses, which requires freedom of mental and physical contraction. The joy of the horse is the ultimate goal.

In our world today, we see two approaches to training horses and the roots are clearly visible in history. The only real question is how to continue. Who do we want to be as riders? As human beings? Are you willing to acknowledge the version of yourself reflected in your horse? Or is there more to learn?

Control or negotiate. Wrestle or dance. Slave or partner. War or love.

With a nod to those good horses retired too young, lost to neglect, and all the horses who paid dearly for our dreams— along with a hope that we will do better for your offspring than we have for you.

Natural Instinct: The Human Half

The more we riders understand about horse instinct, the better. Instinct is the starting place; a behavioral baseline from which all other trained behaviors are built. So we study wild horses to find out what their language is like, how they experience family dynamics, and what it means to be a prey animal. We humans like things in tidy piles, so we label and over-simplify behaviors. Most are negative piles, like Arabians are spooky or Thoroughbreds are hot. It's about as logical as saying Colorado riders are heavy-handed.

We love to break herd dominance down into a grudge hierarchy from alpha mare down to older gelding, because the view is easier in extremes. But looking at the lowest common denominator is deceptive. The old adage says that the alpha horse eats first. In captivity, it could be the ulcer horse who is more food aggressive, but we miss that message. I recently read a study that says in the wild, horses don't compete for food, even in low availability situations. They cooperate.

Instead of watching what makes horses different from each other, it would benefit riders to study the ways in which the herd works together, as a behavioral lesson for our partnership with them. Horses understand that they're safer and stronger if they work together. One of my personal favorite herd behaviors is easy to see in August. Commonly horses are standing quiet, side by side and heads nuzzled close to a herdmate's hind quarters, while tails flick loosely, working to move each other's flies away.

The larger the group, the closer they stand, breathing together and peacefully creating a breeze for each other. This vision of cooperation is what we should emulate.

But even if our understanding of horse temperament is balanced and takes individuality into account, it's still only half the picture. What about our own instincts?

First, we're predators. Our eyes are close together. We literally see everything differently. We're bi-peds with opposable thumbs. Add to that the habit we have of asking babies to grab onto our fingers as soon as they are born; we are a species that uses hands for communication and control.

Where horses are ruled by their senses, we are ruled by our intellect. Our thoughts distract us from the natural world, and our senses are not very acute in the first place, compared to other mammals. The over-simplification of this is that we think and horses feel. We are one step removed from the physical world and when animals tell us something about that world, we don't see or hear it as quickly. We use our brains to call them spooky, discrediting their frequently-correct perception, while affirming our reason. In the worst case, we are degrading their confidence while being arrogant about our own.

Horses are kind of spherical in dominance ranking. Within the herd, there are friendships and preferences rather than a hard, fast top-to-bottom list. Too many humans relate to a horse as a black and white, right or wrong situation—that's more about control than partnership. Blunt dominance is a kind of disrespect, by its nature, while partnership is more complex.

Horses and humans are both challenged to stay balanced when we carry weight on our backs. We do have that in common.

For us humans, we bring two other ingredients that are nearly combustible. First, we have passion. Desire is like pouring gasoline on a fire. We rush and hurry and if we don't get an answer fast enough, we ask again, louder this time. Ambition about the future clouds the immediate view. We surrender awareness in the moment and look to the end result, without involving a step-by-step path to get there happily. We see ourselves cantering rhythmically with our horses but we don't know how to get them there without a fight.

But that dilemma is tiny compared to this last ingredient needed for riding. Horses use their senses intuitively, yet nothing we do in the saddle is intuitive. Learning to ride is challenging because there is no part of it that comes naturally. Everything is a paradox. Staying in the saddle looks like sitting still, but bracing into the saddle actually pushes us out of it. Fluidity in the sit-bones equates to stillness, because what *appears* as stillness is actually us moving in unison with the horse. That's the challenge of sitting the trot.

Common sense tells us that if the horse bolts, hold on with your legs, but that's their cue to go forward. We think we can control horse movements with our hands, but they listen to our bodies. Our muscle tension translates our true feelings, ones that we aren't honest enough to admit to, while we think horses should be ruled by human logic.

Horses inhabit each hair on their body while we have little body awareness. And it's just like a human to judge someone else's behavior rather than take control of their own. Most telling, on these hot August days, when a horse reaches to shoosh a fly, we pull that bit, metal on bone, to "correct" them.

And finally, horses are flight animals and we like to stand and fight.

Could we possibly be a worse match? We act like braggarts and monsters. Do we have any innate partner skills or are we control freaks? Our best weapon is compassion, but who trains that?

On the other side of the balance, horses offer one princely gift. They volunteer to join up with us. They reach out, even when afraid; even if humans in the past have been thoughtless or cruel. Still they offer their noble, sentient selves as partners. Perhaps they see even more possibility in us than we do in them.

Dressage Factions and the Real Reason to Compete

I'm a traditionalist when it comes to the art of dressage. I love the structure, the fundamentals, the words of the classical masters. Dressage is the peaceful partnering of a horse and rider in a dance. It's a discipline of intuition, subtle cues, and long term goals; a relationship that's forged by patience and time. Dressage is freedom of expression within limitation; a waltz, a sonnet, a bird in flight.

The modern world hasn't improved on dressage. Like every other riding discipline, some of us mistakenly train harder, faster, and younger. Some horses are enslaved by dominance; money is given priority over art and time. So it goes; humans are an imperfect species.

Now there are different versions of dressage; dressage in Eventing, as well as Western Dressage, Cowboy Dressage, and a few lesser knowns. It's all good as long as it's held to the same beautiful standards of balance, relaxation, and responsiveness. The more horses being ridden to these ideals, the better. I'm still a traditionalist but being inclusive just makes sense for horses.

The bicker-fest I dislike the most is between proponents of competitive dressage vs classical dressage. I also think it's the silliest. There, I said it.

Competitive dressage is famously the home of rollkur (hyper-flexion of the horse's neck achieved through aggressive force), a practice that's common in western disciplines like reining as well. There are always bad apples, but when I see rollkur, I think it's a sure sign that the rider has lost himself and given up on his horse. I hate rollkur but it's wrong to name-call all competitors, as if rollkur was the standard majority opinion; as if most riders showing their horses are wicked. It's just not fair or true.

The other extreme is classical dressage, claiming the high moral ground. They pridefully decry every competitive rider infraction, judging others harshly from the rail, while never putting their principles to the test. They see any competition as ugly, while they rise above it all—riding only for themselves. The practice of any art becomes elitist when kept in a hot-house.

Again, I'm a traditionalist, but I don't like separation. I believe fighting between factions only makes us weaker. Dressage is a tradition that has survived centuries for a reason. It's a mistake to judge any discipline by the worst expression of it, whether it's on a jumbo-tron or in a back pasture.

The most frequent complaint about competitive dressage is that the fundamentals aren't rewarded. That horses ridden behind the bit, even at the lowest levels, get rewarded by judges while others, riding in a more correct, compassionate way, don't get rewarded. The problem with this opinion is that, taken at face value, it means the best of us are staying home, giving ground to riders more interested in a particular look than the welfare of their horse. They will take over our sport if we stay home and whine about it. Hold your ground and let your voice be heard!

If dressage is the perfect riding discipline, as I believe it is, then trust it. Do the work and trust that your horse, in time, will be the best advertisement for kind, perceptive training. Trust dressage to shine through.

Fact: There are plenty of elite dressage competitors who visibly uphold kind training traditions and they deserve your support. Rollkur is not the majority opinion. Fact: The vast majority of members of the United States Dressage Federation are adult amateur riders at training or first level. It's *your* organization and if you don't like the way it's going, use your voice to make it better. Then get a group of like-minds together and stake your claim in some temporary stalls at a show. Don't let your corner of the horse world be sold out to haters.

Aside from politics, is there a reason to show a horse? Being competitive isn't a dirty word but how many of us feel uncomfortable about it? It's a complicated question for women on our culture. Rest the politics and the emotional baggage—just ride your horse. It's okay to not consider yourself a competitive person. Truth be told, it's an advantage.

Once we manage to tame our egos, this might be the best reason to show a horse: It's relationship out of the box, on someone else's time schedule, on unfamiliar turf. It says that your horse is adaptable, willing, and a good sport to join you. It means that you believed in your horse, as he believed in you. It's an act of trust to ask to agree to be looked at and then deal with the consequences; to take a risk together and invite the world to watch.

There will be ribbons in a range of colors with placings noted and records kept. Ribbons aren't worth much more than that; they're only a symbol. It's your partnership that mattered. That the two of you spent weekends challenging yourselves to improve, always competing against your last show, and balancing winning and losing into a place of faith and trust. That the two of you built a special relationship that made a difference, if not in the huge world, certainly in your own hearts. You persevered through joy and pain, thrill and dread, and in the end, there was a place that the two of your shared. Ribbons say it was worth celebrating. In a world where horses struggle, suffer, and die for the whims of humans, it says that you saw past the surface and shared breath and heart with another soul. You lifted your eyes higher.

No, competition isn't necessary. And those who don't

challenge this particular obstacle are no less committed partners with their horses. And in the end, it's all the same—we
loved every minute, even the hard ones.

But maybe like me, you have a huge box of ribbons in the
garage that take up space with old prom dresses and suitcases
that took trips. Maybe the horses have passed on but the faded
ribbons remain. It's still something.

Listening with Your Seat

How's your derrière? Is posterior a more delicate word than rump? Our culture has a lot of fanny chatter: too flat, too round, somehow sagging. Riders should care less about the superficial *do these white breeches make my butt look big?* and more about how does my backside feel...to the horse, obviously. We aspire to evolve our seat.

The dressage master, Nuno Oliveira, had what some thought to be the most profound seat on a horse. He rode hunched over during the last years of his life and yet he became a better rider, his horses were also more relaxed and brilliant.

A *profound* seat...rather than controlling his horse, it unleashed brilliance. What an inspiration.

Gaining skill as a rider starts with acquiring a good level of relaxation in the mind and then allowing that to spread through our body, eventually starting to put positive energy in the seat area to work toward a deeper seat.

A more sensitive seat is the crucial step between being a dominating rider and a perceptive, communicative rider.

We all start riding by wanting to make the horse do something, even if it's only walking away from the herd. We have a picture in our heads and we go to work—pushing, pulling, kicking. Maybe you think you are a quiet rider, whose hands don't jerk but instead you just pull, adding a pound of pressure as your horse does, until it's a full-out tug-o-war. Even if your pressure is passive-aggressive, it's still adversarial. About then emotions get involved and things get worse. We are so focused on having our way that we don't listen. That's what domination is.

Listening to a horse, to be literal, does not involve your ears. Yes, they may snort or blow, but the larger area (no pun intended) of communication is always through the part of us most connected to the horse; our seat positions us spine-to-spine with the horse, nervous system to nervous system. In order to evolve a deeper, more aware seat while in the saddle, a rider must quiet the mental chatter, relax the actual gluteal muscles, and become internally aware of how the horse physically feels between our legs.

Put delicately, riding is the process of getting our brains out of our heads and into our behinds. It means less brain-thinking, even if it's about hand position and cuing transitions. We are searching for feel, for finesse, and that's a sensual awareness, not an intellectual opinion.

A mentally dominating rider uses a horse like a dirt bike, revving the engine and slamming the chassis to and fro attempting to meet a requirement. The rider is talking with herself about how to make the horse do something and leaving the most important thing out: the horse. Whether the rider is angry or just quietly frustrated, it's still a fight because it starts with two sides, each alone and distanced. It's like trying to learn the tango by counting the beat and looking down watching your tense, reluctant feet. When the dance happens through mental math, there is no fluidity. No romance.

Dressage riders can appear to have a glazed look sometimes. While a jumper is turning and looking for the next jump, a dressage rider seems almost in a trance of mental stillness, even as the horse performing shoulder-in or flying changes. They glide along effortlessly with no resistance. The secret is that the more intense the work gets, the smaller the cues become, so the horse and rider seem to move as one.

Disclaimer: Moving as one with a horse sounds mystical, but

it isn't. It's a give and take of perception between partners. It isn't about right or wrong, but rather a physical awareness of a small tension in the neck, or a slight lean of a shoulder. It could be either the horse or the rider, but when noticed so early, the partner's response can be a small, subtle suggestion—peaceful and rhythmic. In other words, it looks like a dance. Maybe when our lumbering and hyperactive brain gets out of the way, our soul can come forward to elevate the connection. You know this is right because horses don't inspire our minds, but our hearts. It's where they live and we have to make our way to them there to be a partner.

Remember, the only means horses have of communicating with us is through their bodies. We are too quick to judge their actions negatively. We correct them when they tell us how they feel. Their feelings are not any more open to debate than ours are. They are eloquent and honest, but our seats must learn to listen and become more responsive. That desire for an enlightened kind of soulmate connection with a horse is never a mental transaction. It's beyond pretense and words, deep in our spines, where truth and spirit are all that matters.

A deep seat means that physically we aren't stiffly perched, but rather relaxed and plugged in, responding fluidly to our horse. Beyond that, deep also means thinking less and feeling more. It's being introspective, discerning, esoteric, and if you rest in that silence long enough, even profound.

My first trainer, who absolutely hated dressage, always told me to "take a deep seat and a faraway look." It's cowboy talk for the same thing.

Permission NOT to Ride

Last Tuesday I had an 8 a.m. lesson with a boarder and her sweet gelding. He's had a good summer; they even made it to a couple of schooling shows. This gelding had a checkered past with several previous owners and when this pair started with me, he was a wild man. The lunge line doubled as a life line back then. But he's been a solid citizen for the last couple of years—honest and responsive. My client has done a wonderful job and the judges rewarded their good work together.

The air was fall-crisp as the three of us walked to the arena. He nickered a bit on the way but once inside, the gelding spun, faced the barn, and the real caterwauling began. We thought it would pass and didn't over-react. I remember thinking as wide as his mouth was open, the bit could practically fall down his throat. We gave him some time… but he elevated it to haunted-house-worthy screaming—a twitchy-eyed-and-quivering-lip wailing. Who is this guy?

The gelding could have been an anomaly, but he wasn't. The next day as I drove up to another barn for a lesson, my client and his sensitive, sweet mare were belly-spinning with fear-glazed eyes and a very humped back. Two other horses in my extended herd of clients are lame from "playing too hard"—both cases left over-night manure piles reduced to confetti. At home, my mare and one of my geldings managed to open the two gates between them. By the time I got out there, my mare swaggered toward me, acting the clear victor, covered with welts and cheese-grater wounds on all sides, while the gelding looked freshly groomed and just out of church.

It's the first week of colder nights with temperatures in the forties. Winter coats are blooming on every rump and the pasture is dead-brown. There's been a change in the wind. The mares are all in raging heat cycles and the flies are all in a death-snit. Yes, it's a huge deal: season change. The barometer rules. Especially if your senses are about two hundred times keener than a human's.

Back in our home arena, my client has the lunge line on her gelding who's bouncing straight up and down, bucking like rank stock, landing stiff-legged, and not one inch ahead of his last hoof prints. We share dubious glances and expect an alien to spring out of his chest any moment now.

On days like this, a question hangs in the air. "Should I ride?" Are you being a wimp if you don't? Or a dominating jerk if you do? Would you cancel a lesson if you had a migraine or a shoulder sprain or another invisible ailment? Would you cancel if your horse was obviously lame?

What do you do when there is a lesson ticking away and you don't recognize the horse on the end of the line? What is his problem? Humans ask why; we need to dissect it and find the cause of the demonic possession. I repeat: He is a sweet, kind, and honest horse. Has he swallowed a chain saw? We don't think he's hurt or sick... and we can guess all day long. The truth is that his behavior is probably a perfect storm of a few things. The cause isn't as important as what we do next.

"You can't let him win." We've all been told that since our first horse. "You have to climb on and ride him through it. If you let him get away with this it will spoil him forever," comes some voice from the past. Never mind that he is using everything he has to tell us that he isn't okay. Never mind that he's an honest horse who doesn't evade work normally. Never mind that you planned a lesson.

A reminder: the only way a horse has to communicate with

us is by using his body. Your frustration complains that he certainly knows better! We'll this gelding does, too… but today is a unique day and I notice there are days that I can't find the bottom of a bucket. What if he isn't being disobedient? Whatever he's trying to tell us is very real to him—he isn't faking his anxiety.

Does your ego demand that he behave right now? Is compassion a sign of weakness? What kind of leader are you when he needs you?

After a bit of lunging, our gelding is moving forward halfheartedly, still watching for the apocalypse. Did I mention he's nineteen this year? In spite of current appearances, their work together is not so fragile. When a horse's emotions get hot, we have to stay cool.

And there's a miracle cure. In dressage, we believe that you get a horse's attention by asking for transitions. So we asked for changes of gait on the line. They weren't pretty, but he got praised for them anyway. Sure enough, they improved, and he gave us a short blow. Then we began to supple him on the lunge line. Most of us don't use lunging to its full purpose. In truth, anything we ask for in the saddle is available while lunging. We put his brain to work with a positive conversation and he soon found his way back to his usual self. The other term for this is building trust. He'll pay us back in the future by showing us grace when we need it.

Your gelding wants you to know that anxiety isn't soothed by harsh discipline. Your mare wants you to know on your worst PMS day, you aren't all that compliant either. Take a breath and relax, human. Ground work is your friend. My advice? If your common sense whispers to stay on the ground, do it with no apology. Ego is never worth an injury, for your horse or yourself.

Besides, you've got plenty of time. Rome didn't burn in a day.

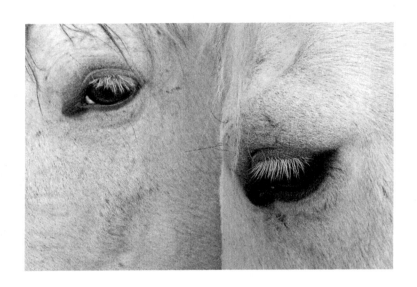

How to Love Horses Forever

We were born this way. It should be part of the Apgar test. It would resolve so much if newborns gave an early warning—just like any other heart condition.

Most of us didn't live around horses in the beginning. We saw them in our first books or from car windows. Or maybe it was cellular memory and we thought we just knew them because it felt like we always had. In the beginning, there was simply nothing easier than loving horses.

We got this far just daydreaming; we were horse-crazy kids cantering around the yard playing horse. Kids who nickered and pranced, loving to feel the wind in our hair and the rhythm of our tennis-shoe-hooves on ground. Maybe a dream horse taught us.

Then we got our first touch; our first shared breath. Maybe we squealed like a siren and flapped our arms to let them know we wanted to fly, but ended up poking them in the eye instead. The deal was struck and it was the first time a horse forgave us, of course, as he would forever. Because he saw a flash of who we might become; because he had as much forgiveness as we had love.

Maybe we were lucky beyond all reason and got to sit on a horse while he was led around. Beware: once that happens, our feet never authentically touch the ground again. And it was all about us. Our love was selfish because the need was too huge to even name. So, another tradition began: we cried mad tears when we had to get off. But old horsewomen watching nodded and considered the outburst good manners. They got misty and nostalgic remembering that their first thank-yous were mad howls, too.

Then one day the heavens opened and we got our first horse. We pushed our noses deep into the mane and the addiction had a smell. Probably more tears, because words are no match for the emotion. It was also the first moment that loving horses got complicated.

We all know this part, too. It was prioritizing money and time. We needed to find a balance while squeezing pieces into a mental pie chart of our lives. We wanted so much and we wouldn't take no for an answer. We were trying to live our personal version of *National Velvet*.

We carried our willful bravado into the saddle. Our love for horses was as fierce as a high-school crush. We wanted to jump or spin or dance; we wanted to ride every day. Our horses tolerated us but we surely hit some walls while training. Some of our horses were bemused with our folly, while the very best horses bucked our arrogant backsides off. These were the character years. We learned how to hit the ground and climb back on. We tried out leadership styles in the saddle, with varying impressions of success. We cared too much what people thought, whether it was the judge or a stranger at the barn. We may have said we didn't want to compete, but we still judged ourselves and our horses without mercy. Whatever goal we had, we tried too hard. And so we had to learn to be good losers before we could win.

Some of us gave up everything for our horses and some of us made a strategic retreat in the name of career or kids. Our parents grew old by the time we caught our breath. The biggest certainty was that we loved horses even when it was impossible.

The view from midlife is bittersweet. Some of our friends have quit riding already. By now we've come off a few times and our bodies remember, even if our minds have repressed it. Our hormones are failing us and it makes us timid. We can't stop apologizing for it.

But at the same time, we can feel how strong our love has made us. Strong enough to shoulder whatever life gave us. Strong enough to say good-bye to old campaigners and strong enough to start over again. Horses have taught us to value the important qualities in ourselves above the superficial: patience and perseverance, creativity and commitment, love and partnership.

And when we have had many days, and our childhood need is almost met, it's more possible to look around and feel the beauty and wonder of this equine journey. To know that the very best part of who we've become was a gift from our horse. Maybe it was what he saw when we were babies and now it's time to come full circle.

How to love a horse is both easy and complicated at this age. Sure, some of us fail our horses without concern, but many more of us grow horse-sized hearts in our chests. Most of us just want to be in the barn. We want to muck until we fall over dead and need mucking up ourselves. We want our bones to bleach out peacefully with our horse's bones.

But we have a debt to pay forward, for all those years of weather-beaten hands and sore bones. All those years of mounted ego-correction eventually taught us to think of another's welfare first. And now that we are less selfish, there's work to be done. There are horse-crazy kids who need us to hold the lead line and tell the story. Or maybe your heart and barn have room for one more un-rideable, homeless old mare. Or maybe after all these years, you've developed an indoor voice for horses, speaking up for the ones who need rescue, just like you did.

What's next for you? The horse love is as fresh and hot as that first day, and it's still your ride.

About the Author

Anna Blake was born in Cavalier County, North Dakota, in 1954. She's a writer, blogger, dressage trainer, and horse advocate, residing at Infinity Farm on the flat, windy, treeless prairie of Colorado. The herd also includes horses, llamas, goats, dogs, cats, and Edgar Rice Burro.

CPSIA information can be obtained
at www.ICGtesting.com
Printed in the USA
LVOW04s0755160616

492863LV00010B/71/P